2nd Edition

Cases and
Applications

Dalton
PfP
Series

Michael A. Dalton, Ph.D., J.D., CPA, CFP, CLU, ChFC
James F. Dalton, MBA, MS, CPA/PFS, CFP

DALTON PUBLICATIONS, L.L.C.

150 James Drive East, Suite 100

St. Rose, Louisiana 70087

(504) 464-9772 • (504) 461-9860 Fax

www.daltonpublications.com

ISBN 1-890260-12-6   **Personal Financial Planning Cases and Applications**

ISBN 1-890260-11-8   Personal Financial Planning Cases and Applications
                      Instructor's Manual

DEDICATION

To the CFP® Registered Programs, their directors, and students who have used and adopted this case book. Their ideas and input have helped make this book a success.

ADDITIONAL PRODUCTS AND SERVICES

Other Products in Our Personal Financial Planning Series:

- Understanding Your Financial Calculator
  James F. Dalton

Products and Services in Our CFP® Examination Review Series:

- Live Instructional Reviews

- Volume I: Outlines and Study Guides, 3rd Edition
  Michael A. Dalton, James F. Dalton, and Cassie F. Bradley

- Volume II: Problems and Solutions, 3rd Edition
  Michael A. Dalton and James F. Dalton

- Volume III: Case Exam Book, 2nd Edition
  Michael A. Dalton, James F. Dalton, and Patricia P. Houlihan

- Mock Exams: Series A, Exams 1 and 2
  Michael A. Dalton and James F. Dalton

- Financial Planning Flashcards
  James F. Dalton and Scott Wasserman

Please contact Dalton Publications for additional information!

150 James Drive East, Suite 100

St. Rose, LA 70087

(504) 464-9772

(504) 461-9860 Fax

http://www.daltonpublications.com

TABLE OF CONTENTS

INTRODUCTION

This textbook is primarily intended for use in a case capstone course for a financial planning curriculum. This textbook can also be used in a specific course such as investments as the questions in each case are identifiable by major topics (i.e., insurance, investments, etc.). This textbook includes thirteen (13) comprehensive financial planning cases. The cases are designed to help the student to integrate the six (6) major areas of personal financial planning:

- Fundamentals of Financial Planning
- Insurance Planning
- Investment Planning
- Income Tax Planning
- Retirement Planning
- Estate Planning

Each case includes a complete family scenario that represents the information the financial planner obtained from the client. Generally, each case scenario includes information obtained from the client in the following sections and order:

- Personal Background and Information
- Personal and Financial Goals
- Economic Information
- Insurance Information
- Investment Information
- Income Tax Information
- Retirement Information

- Gifts, Estates, Trusts, and Will Information
- Statement of Cash Flows
- Statement of Financial Position
- Information Regarding Assets and Liabilities
- Exhibits

Each case contains between 24 and 57 questions covering the major areas of financial planning.

Many of the cases have exhibits to add a sense of reality to the case. The exhibits include actual wills, trusts, SSA 7004, investment statements, etc. Most of the cases have one or more documents designed to familiarize the student with an actual example of such documents.

The textbook contains six (6) appendixes that should greatly assist the student in answering the questions and analyzing the cases. The appendixes are divided into the six major areas of personal financial planning. The following exhibits are included:

Appendix	Major Financial Planning Area	Number of Exhibits	Brief Description of Exhibits
A	Fundamentals	1	House Costs and Debt Repayment
B	Insurance	5	Ratings of Companies • Life Insurance Policy Replacement • Homeowners Policy Summary • Covered Perils • Eight General Exclusions
C	Investments	10	Total, Unsystematic, and Systematic Risks • Call and Put Options • Rates of Return • Standard Deviation • Performance Measurements • Formulas
D	Income Tax	6	Tax Rates and Brackets • Exemptions and Deductions • Credits • Sections 79 and 179
E	Retirement	13	Defined Benefit and Defined Contribution Plans • Keoghs • Annuities • Single Life Expectancy • Self-Employed Person's Rate
F	Estates	6	Probate Assets • Unified Tax Rates • Gift Tax and Estate Formulas • Trust

These exhibits provide the student with information within the textbook to answer many of the questions asked without referring back to another textbook or source.

THE CASE METHOD

The clear objective of this case book is to prepare competent financial planners through the simulated practice of answering comprehensive questions.

Personal financial planning case analysis is the process used to formulate financial recommendations for clients given their clients' current situation, expectations, and goals. Case analysis provides students with practice in bringing experience, theory, and common sense to bear in the formulation of plans and recommendations in realistic situations.

The case method class structure differs from the traditional lecture class structure in that the students must take a more active role in the learning process. The student must determine the problem, select the appropriate tools, and formulate a plan, all in the absence of full and complete information. Additionally, the student will be faced with the fact that often there is no one, best plan of action. These complications are indicative of what a personal financial planner faces in the "real world."

While each student is unique and each case is different, the authors suggest that students develop a basic approach to analyzing cases. In reviewing the case scenario, the student will find it useful to briefly read the case scenario to get a feel for the clients and the overall case. Then, the student should reread the case in detail, making written notes to assure an in-depth comprehension of the case situation. The student may wish to subdivide the issues into the six (6) major areas of personal financial planning:

- Fundamentals of Financial Planning
- Insurance Planning
- Investment Planning
- Income Tax Planning
- Retirement Planning
- Estate Planning

The student should begin by identifying the strengths and weaknesses of the financial situation presented by the client in each area. It is important not to confuse symptoms with problems or to make premature evaluations. The student will often find that a problem in one area is related to and complicated by a problem in another area.

Once the student has a thorough understanding of the case situation and has begun to identify areas of concern, the student should then focus on answering the specific questions presented at the end of the case. With practice, the student should become more proficient in identifying the issues presented in the questions even before reading the questions. A thorough understanding of the case information will help to direct the student to both questions and answers.

Many of the questions direct the student to review the current or proposed situation and evaluate the appropriateness, effectiveness, soundness, or validity of such a situation. In the evaluation process, the student will need to understand the consequences of each decision and be able to suggest possible alternatives taking into consideration known and even unknown information. It is always important to keep in mind that it is the function of the personal financial planner to help the client optimize his/her situation in order to plan for both the present and future needs, as well as the objectives of the client.

The student should keep two important things in mind. The information the authors have presented for each of these cases is probably more complete and better organized than that which the usual client in practice presents to the professional financial planner. Furthermore, while ratios are intended to generate questions and to focus attention, they are not a perfect tool. By utilizing a variety of ratio measures, the student should get a pretty good idea of debt management, savings rate, financial security, and progress towards financial security in retirement.

ACKNOWLEDGMENTS AND SPECIAL THANKS

We appreciate the tremendous support and encouragement we have received from everyone throughout the development of this project. We are extremely grateful to the users of our texts who provided us with valuable comments concerning our first edition.

This manual would not have been possible without the extraordinary efforts and dedication of the following:

- Scott Wasserman and Gilbert Araiza, who reviewed each case scenario, question, and answer for technical accuracy.
- David Durr, who reviewed selected case scenarios, questions, and answers for technical accuracy.
- Tammy Clifton, who reviewed each case scenario, question, and answer for grammatical accuracy.
- Marguerite Merritt and Allison Dalton, who reviewed selected case scenarios, questions, and answers for grammatical accuracy.
- Connie Powell, Donna Dalton, and Kristi Mincher who co-managed the project and incorporated most of the revisions into the 2nd Edition.
- Michelle Bonnette, Tina Collins, Alayne Copes, Robin Delle, Wendy Doerr, and Jan Marlbrough who helped with revisions, formatting, and proofing.
- Our families and friends for their support and assistance.

We have received so much help, from so many people; it is possible that we inadvertently overlooked thanking someone. If so, it is our shortcoming and we apologize in advance. Please let us know if you are that someone and we will correct it in our next printing.

ABOUT THE AUTHORS

Michael A. Dalton, Ph.D., JD, CPA, CFP, CLU, ChFC

- Associate professor of Accounting and Taxation at Loyola University in New Orleans, Louisiana
- Ph.D. in Accounting from Georgia State University
- J.D. from Louisiana State University in Baton Rouge, Louisiana
- MBA and BBA in Management and Accounting from Georgia State University
- Former board member of the CFP® Board of Standards and Board of Governors
- Former chairman of the CFP® Board of Examiners
- Conducted in-house financial planning and training courses for Exxon corporation, ITT, Federal Express, the New Orleans Saints, and Chrysler Corporation
- Co-author of *Dalton CFP® Examination Review - Volume I and II, 1st, 2nd, and 3rd Edition, Dalton CFP® Examination Review Mock Exams A-1 and A-2, CPA Review and Cost Accounting: Traditions and Innovations*, and *ABCs of Managing Your Money*
- Member of the Editorial Review Board for the *Journal of Financial Planning*

James F. Dalton, MBA, MS, CPA/PFS, CFP

- Manager with an international accounting firm, specializing in Personal Financial Planning and investment consulting
- MBA from Loyola University in New Orleans, Louisiana
- Masters of Accounting in Taxation from the University of New Orleans
- BS in accounting from Florida State University in Tallahassee, Florida
- Completed two of three levels of CFA Examination
- Member of the CFP® Board of Standards July 1996, Comprehensive CFP® Exam Pass Score Committee
- Member of the AICPA and the Louisiana Society of CPAs
- Author of *Understanding Your Financial Calculator*
- Co-author of *Dalton CFP® Examination Review - Volumes I and II, 1st, 2nd, and 3rd Edition, Dalton CFP® Examination Review Mock Exams A-1 and A-2,* and *Financial Planning Flashcards*

IKE AND RHONDA SUMRALL

CASE SCENARIO AND QUESTIONS

IKE AND RHONDA SUMRALL

Table of Contents

IKE AND RHONDA SUMRALL

Case Scenario and Questions

Today is January 1, 1999. Ike and Rhonda Sumrall have come to you, a financial planner, for help in developing a plan to accomplish their financial goals. From your initial meeting together, you have gathered the following information:

PERSONAL BACKGROUND AND INFORMATION

Ike Sumrall (Age 27)

Ike is an assistant in the marketing department for EnergyTech, Inc. His annual salary is $26,000.

Rhonda Sumrall (Age 24)

Rhonda is a legal research assistant with the law firm of Glennon, Gerald & Powell, L.L.C. Her annual salary is $20,000.

The Children

Ike and Rhonda have no children from this marriage. Ike has two children, Jake (Age 4) and Sam (Age 3), from a former marriage. Jake and Sam live with their mother, Judy.

The Sumralls

Ike and Rhonda have been married for two years.

Ike must pay $325 per month in child support until both Sam and Jake reach age 18. The divorce decree also requires Ike to create an insurance trust for the benefit of the children and contribute $175 per month to the trustee. The trustee is Judy's father. There are no withdrawal powers on the part of the beneficiaries. The trust is to be used for the education and/or maintenance of the children in the event of Ike's death. The trustee has the power to invade any trust principal for the beneficiaries at the earlier of the death of Ike or Sam reaching age 18.

PERSONAL AND FINANCIAL OBJECTIVES

1. Save for an emergency fund.

2. Eliminate all consumer debt.

3. Save for a 20% down payment on their dream house. The current value of the house is $100,000.   Property taxes would be $1,200, and insurance would be $750.   Both taxes and insurance are expected to increase with inflation.

4. Contribute to tax advantaged savings.

5. Plan to have additional children in seven years.

ECONOMIC INFORMATION

- Inflation is expected to be 4.0% annually.

- Their salaries should increase 5.0% for the next five to ten years.

- No state income tax.

- Slow growth economy; stocks are expected to grow at 9.5%.

Bank lending rates are as follows:

- 15-year mortgage 7.5%.

- 30-year mortgage 8.0%.

- Secured personal loan 10.0%.

INSURANCE INFORMATION

Life Insurance

	Policy A	Policy B	Policy C
Insured	Ike	Ike	Rhonda
Face Amount	$250,000	$78,000[2]	$20,000
Type	Whole Life	Group Term	Group Term
Cash Value	$2,000	$0	$0
Annual Premium	$2,100	$178	$50
Who pays premium	Trustee	Employer	Employer
Beneficiary	Trustee[1]	Judy	Ike
Policy Owner	Trust	Ike	Rhonda
Settlement options clause selected	None	None	None

[1] Sam and Jake are beneficiaries of the trust.

[2] This was increased from $50,000 to $78,000 January 1, 1999.

Health Insurance

Ike and Rhonda are covered under Ike's employer plan which is an indemnity plan with a $200 deductible per person per year and an 80/20 major medical co-insurance clause with a family annual stop loss of $1,500.

Long-Term Disability Insurance

Ike is covered by an "own occupation" policy with premiums paid by his employer. The benefits equal 60% of his gross pay after an elimination period of 180 days. The policy covers both sickness and accidents and is guaranteed renewable.

Rhonda is not covered by disability insurance.

Renters Insurance

The Sumralls have a HO4 renters policy without endorsements.

Content Coverage $25,000; Liability $100,000.

Automobile Insurance

Both Car and Truck*

Type	PAP
Bodily Injury	$25,000/$50,000
Property Damage	$10,000
Medical Payments	$5,000 per person
Physical Damage	Actual Cash Value
Uninsured Motorist	$25,000/$50,000
Comprehensive Deductible	$200
Collision Deductible	$500
Premium (annual)	$3,300

*They do not have any additional insurance on Rhonda's motorcycle.

INVESTMENT INFORMATION

The Sumralls think that they need six months of cash flow net of all taxes, savings, vacation, and discretionary cash flow in an emergency fund. They are willing to include in the emergency fund the savings account and Ike's 401(k) balance because it has borrowing provisions.

The Federal Express stock was a gift to Ike from his Uncle Joe. At the date of the gift (July 1, 1990), the fair market value of the stock was $3,500. Uncle Joe's tax basis was $2,500, and Uncle Joe paid gift tax of $1,400 on the gift. Uncle Joe had already used up both his unified credit and annual exclusion to Ike.

The K&B stock was a gift to Rhonda last Christmas of 100 shares from her Uncle Mike. At the date of the gift (December 25, 1998) the fair market value was $8,000 and Mike had paid $10,000 for the stock in 1992 (his tax basis).

The Growth Mutual Fund (currently valued at $13,900) had been acquired by Ike over the years 1993, 1994, 1995, 1996, 1997, and 1998 with deposits of $1,000, $1,000, $2,000, $2,000, $2,500 and $3,000. The earnings were all reinvested and Ike received 1099s for the income and capital gains during the years of earnings ($0/1993, $200/1994, $400/1995, $400/1996, $650/1997, $750/1998).

INCOME TAX INFORMATION

The filing status of the Sumralls for Federal income tax is married filing jointly. Both the children (Sam and Jake) are claimed as dependents on the Sumrall's tax return as part of the divorce agreement. The Sumralls live in a state that does not have state income tax.

Section 79 Limit on Premium Schedule
Age 29 and under $0.08 per month/per $1,000.

RETIREMENT INFORMATION

Ike currently contributes 3% of his salary to his 401(k). The employer matches each $1 contributed with $0.50 up to a total employer contribution of 3% of salary.

GIFTS, ESTATES, TRUSTS, AND WILL INFORMATION

Ike has a will leaving all of his probate estate to his children.

Rhonda does not have a will.

The Sumralls live in a common law state that has adopted the Uniform Probate Code.

STATEMENT OF CASH FLOWS

Ike and Rhonda Sumrall
Statement of Cash Flows (Expected to be similar in 1999)
January 1, 1998 - December 31, 1998

CASH INFLOWS
Salaries
Ike-Salary	$26,000	
Rhonda-Salary	20,000	
Investment Income*	1,090	
Total Inflows		**$47,090**

CASH OUTFLOWS
Savings-House down payment	$ 1,200	
Reinvestment of Investment Income	1,090	
401(k) Contribution	780	
Total Savings		**$ 3,070**

FIXED OUTFLOWS
Child Support	$ 3,900	
Life Insurance Payment (To Trustee)	2,100	
Rent	6,600	
Renters Insurance	480	
Utilities	720	
Telephone	360	
Auto payment P&I as of 1/1/99	3,600	
Auto Insurance	3,300	
Gas, Oil, Maintenance	2,400	
Student loans	3,600	
Credit Card Debt	1,800	
Furniture payments	1,302	
Total Fixed Outflows		**$30,162**

VARIABLE OUTFLOWS
Taxes-Ike FICA	$ 1,989	
Taxes-Rhonda FICA	1,530	
Taxes-Federal Tax Withheld	4,316	
Food	3,600	
Clothing	1,000	
Entertainment/Vacation	1,500	
Total Variable Outflows		**$13,935**
Total Cash Outflows		**$47,167**
Discretionary Cash Flows (negative)		**$ (77)**
TOTAL CASH OUTFLOWS		**$47,090**

*$340 from dividends and $750 from other investment sources.

STATEMENT OF FINANCIAL POSITION

Ike and Rhonda Sumrall
Balance Sheet
As of January 1, 1999

ASSETS[1]   LIABILITIES & NET WORTH

Cash and Equivalents   **Liabilities[2]**
Cash $ 500   Credit Card balance VISA $ 9,000
Savings Account   1,000   Credit Card balance M/C   0
Total Cash and Equivalents $1,500   Student Loan-Ike[4]   45,061
                                             Auto Loan-Rhonda   14,796
Invested Assets   Furniture Loan   1,533
Fed. Exp. Stock (100 Shares)[3] $ 5,000   *Total Liabilities* $70,390
K&B Stock (100 shares)   7,200
Growth Mutual Fund   13,900
401(k) Account   1,500   **Net Worth**   (46)
Total Invested Assets $27,600

Use Assets
Auto-Rhonda $18,494
Truck-Ike   4,000
Motorcycle - Rhonda   1,000
Personal Property & Furniture   17,750
Total Use Of Assets $41,244
Total Assets $70,344   **Total Liabilities & Net Worth** $70,344

Notes to Financial Statements:
1 Assets are stated at fair market value.
2 Liabilities are stated at principal only as of January 1, 1999 before January payments.
3 Federal Express' current dividend is $3.40.
4 Ike's parents took out the student loans, but he is repaying them.

INFORMATION REGARDING ASSETS AND LIABILITIES

Home Furnishings

The furniture was purchased with 20% down and 18% interest over 36 months. The monthly payment is $108.46.

Automobile

The automobile was purchased January 1, 1999 for $18,494 with 20% down and 80% financed over 60 months with payments of $300 per month.

Stereo System

The Sumralls have a fabulous stereo system (FMV $10,000). They asked and received permission to alter the apartment to build speakers into every room. The agreement with the landlord requires the Sumralls to leave the speakers if they move because the speakers are permanently installed and affixed to the property. The replacement value of the installed speakers is $4,500, and the non-installed components are valued at $5,500. The cost of the system was $10,000, and it was purchased in late 1998.

QUESTIONS

1.   List the Sumralls' financial strengths and weaknesses.

   a.   Strengths:

   b.   Weaknesses:

2.   After reading the case, what additional information would you request from the Sumralls to complete your data-gathering phase?

3.   Calculate the following financial ratios for the Sumralls.

$$\frac{\text{Liquid Assets}}{\text{Monthly Expenses}} \quad =$$

$$\frac{\text{Liquid Assets}}{\text{Current Debt Payments}} \quad =$$

$$\frac{\text{Net Worth}}{\text{Total Assets}} \quad =$$

$$\frac{\text{Total Debt}}{\text{Total Assets}} \quad =$$

$$\frac{\text{Total Debt}}{\text{Annual Gross Income*}} \quad =$$

$$\frac{\text{Annual Housing \& Debt Payments}}{\text{Annual Gross Income}} \quad =$$

$$\frac{\text{Annual Housing Costs}}{\text{Annual Gross Income}} \quad =$$

$$\frac{\text{Investment Assets}}{\text{Annual Gross Income}} \quad =$$

$$\frac{\text{Annual Savings}}{\text{Annual Gross Income}} \quad =$$

*Annual Total Income used in text is the same as gross income.

4.   Comment on any of the above ratios that you think are important.

5.   Describe the Sumralls' current financial condition.

6.   If Ike and Rhonda sell the K&B stock on January 1, 1999 for the fair market value, what are the tax consequences in 1999?

7.   Assuming that Ike and Rhonda decide to sell the Federal Express stock
        on January 15, 1999, for a total price of $5,500, what are the tax
        consequences of such a sale?

8.   How many payments have been made on the furniture purchased as of
        January 1, 1999?

9.   Calculate the original purchase price of the furniture.

10.   What does "guaranteed renewable" mean with regard to the disability
        policy?

11.   Does Rhonda need long-term disability insurance? If so, how much?

12.   If the Sumralls wanted to cover their personal property for replacement
        value, what would they need to do?

13.   If the Sumralls were burglarized and had their movable stereo system components stolen, would it be covered under the HO4 policy, and if so, for what value?

14.   If there were a fire in the Sumralls' apartment building and their in-wall speaker system was destroyed, would they be covered under the HO4 policy, and if so, to what extent?

15.   If a fire forced the Sumralls to move out of their apartment for a month, would the HO4 policy provide any coverage?

16.   Is Rhonda covered for liability on her motorcycle under the PAP?

17.   What is the approximate 1998 Federal tax liability for the Sumralls? Will they have to pay or will they receive a refund?

18.   How much more money do Ike and Rhonda have to save to meet their emergency fund objective?

19.   If the Sumralls sell the Growth Mutual Fund for the statement of financial position value as of January 1, 1999, what will be the tax consequences?

20.   Assuming that the Sumralls plan to buy their dream house seven years from now and expect housing costs to increase at the same rate as the general price index, how much will they have to save at the end of each month to make the down payment if they plan to invest in a broad portfolio of common stocks?

21.   Do the payments of $175 a month to the trustee of the insurance trust for the children constitute a taxable gift?

22.   Who will actually collect the proceeds of Ike's term life insurance, if he were to die today, given that the Sumralls live in a Uniform Probate Code state?

23.   Do the Sumralls presently qualify for a home loan of $80,000 assuming they had a $20,000 down payment and good credit?

24.   Ike is considering borrowing from his 401(k) which has a loan provision. What are the requirements for such a loan?

25.   How much must Ike's employer include in Ike's W-2 for 1999 for the group term life insurance?

26.   Ike and Rhonda are contemplating contributing to IRAs in 1999. What do you tell them?

27.   Ike is trying to determine which is the better choice - the traditional IRA or the Roth IRA. What do you recommend?

28.   What is the implied growth rate of the Federal Express dividend based on
        the constant growth dividend model? Assume that the Sumrall's required
        rate of return is 10%.

CHRISTOPHER AND TIFFANY WHITE

CASE SCENARIO AND QUESTIONS

CHRISTOPHER AND TIFFANY WHITE

Table of Contents

CHRISTOPHER AND TIFFANY WHITE

Case Scenario and Questions

Christopher and Tiffany White have great aspirations for their future. They have only recently realized that they are not as financially well off as they had thought. They have come to you for advice on how to solve their current cash flow problems and to help them plan to achieve future goals. Today is January 1, 1999.

PERSONAL BACKGROUND AND INFORMATION

Christopher White *(Age 30)*

Christopher White graduated from State University with a Bachelor of Science degree in accounting. He has been employed for almost seven years at Blune & Peeron, a small accounting firm (50 employees).

Christopher has been married to Tiffany Kallenborn White for six years.

Tiffany Kallenborn White *(Age 29)*

Tiffany Kallenborn White grew up in a wealthy family and expected to live her married life the same way. While in college, she was crowned Miss State. She graduated from Private University with a Bachelor of Science degree in elementary education. She is employed as a fourth grade teacher at Ridgewood Preparatory private school. To further enrich her students (and for additional income), Tiffany tutors three students per week.

Children

Christopher and Tiffany have three children: John (age 4) and twin girls, Ashley and Allison (age 1½).

Consuela Rodriguez

The Whites employ a young Brazilian student, Consuela Rodriguez to care for their children. Consuela, 21 years old, is a part-time night student at a local community college. She cares for the children and cleans the house in exchange for room, board, and a $100 stipend per week. The Whites pay Consuela in cash. This money is not reported to the IRS by the Whites or Consuela. Consuela works 48 weeks per year.

Christopher's Family

Jonathon White married Bertha Louisa Sanchez White in 1962. They had two children, Jonathon, Jr., and Christopher. Jonathon, Jr. died at six months of age of Sudden Infant Death Syndrome.

Christopher's father, Jonathon, Sr., died from a heart attack six years ago at age 49. He had ample insurance to cover all medical and funeral expenses.

His mother Bertha Louisa, a chain smoker of 37 years, is 53 years old. She was diagnosed with lung cancer three years ago. Due to her rapidly deteriorating condition, her doctor has predicted that she probably will not live beyond five to seven years. Luckily, she has been accepted to receive chemotherapy treatment at The Medical Center ($200 per visit required twice a month).

Her doctor has recommended that she be placed in a home with 24-hour attention as soon as possible. The cost of this care, including room and board, is about $175 per day, or approximately $5,323 per month. Due to her increased medical expenses and need for constant attention, Bertha Louisa has decided to sell her home. She has contacted Gertrude Gardner, a real estate agent, who has listed her home for $71,000. Bertha Louisa is adamant that she will accept no less than $68,000.

Christopher and Tiffany have been giving Bertha Louisa $100 per month to help ease her financial burden. They will be forced to incur most of her future expenses. However, they realize that the sale of the home will provide some assistance. Unfortunately, the real estate market is soft, and they have had no offers on the house.

Tiffany's Family

William Kallenborn, III married Heather Radcliffe Kallenborn in 1961. After years of unsuccessful attempts to have a child, they were pleasantly surprised to find out that Heather was pregnant. Tiffany is an only child and the Kallenborns' pride and joy.

William Kallenborn is a highly respected Supreme Court Justice. He has worked in the city for over 30 years and is considered an extremely influential figure in the community.

Heather Radcliffe was born into an excessively wealthy family. Before they were married, she and William decided that she would not work. She is, however, very active in the community through her volunteer work four days a week.

The Kallenborns were happy to finally welcome Christopher into their family. In fact, William was so excited that he presented Christopher with a speedboat in hopes that he would get to spend time getting to know his future son-in-law. As a wedding gift, the Kallenborns gave Tiffany and Christopher $20,000 towards the purchase of a new home.

In addition, the Kallenborns set up a $100,000 trust fund to assist their grandchildren with college education. Tiffany, the beneficiary of the trust fund, receives the monthly interest from the principal until the trust is dissolved. Upon John's enrollment in college, he will be given his third of the trust fund, $33,333. Tiffany will continue to receive the interest on the remaining $66,666 until Ashley and Allison begin college. If a child should die or decide not to go to college by age 22, that child's share would be donated to Children's Hospital.

Paternity Suit

Despite his love for Tiffany, a drunken Christopher had a one-night stand with Amber Dawn, a local cocktail waitress. Christopher was too ashamed to ever admit this to Tiffany, who was miles away at the time. Shortly after, Christopher heard through one of his friends that Amber had moved to Florida to live with her grandmother.

In December 1997, Christopher was contacted by Perry Mason, Amber Dawn's attorney. Mr. Mason informed Christopher that Amber was claiming that Christopher was the biological father of her 7-year-old daughter, Chrissy. Blood tests and DNA tests have proven this claim to be true.

As the daughter of a Supreme Court Justice, Tiffany has always been in the public eye. The threat of bad publicity forced Christopher to want to settle as quickly as possible. An out of court agreement was reached. Christopher will provide Amber Dawn with payments of $200 per month until Chrissy is 18. Payments began January 1, 1998. Christopher, trying to save his family embarrassment, requested that his only involvement with Chrissy be a monthly check. Amber Dawn, engaged to be married, was happy that Christopher did not want to take active involvement in child rearing. Amber and Christopher entered into an agreement in writing that the $200 could never increase.

Although the out of court settlement was finalized with ease, relations with Tiffany's parents were shaky. It seems that Tiffany's parents were so publicly embarrassed, they could not imagine their daughter still married to this man. They strongly encouraged divorce, offering to provide Tiffany with any financial assistance needed to get out on her own. Tiffany's decision to stand by Christopher through this ordeal resulted in disownment by her parents.

PERSONAL AND FINANCIAL OBJECTIVES

In reviewing a listing of general financial objectives, the Whites list the following financial objectives in direct order of importance to their family (i.e., the item numbered 1 has the highest priority and the item numbered 8 has the lowest):

1. Provide private education for all three children at Ridgewood Preparatory for grades K - 12.
2. Provide each child with up to $15,000 per year for college education for up to four years.
3. Assist Bertha Louisa with living and medical expenses until the time of her death.
4. Purchase a five-bedroom home for $175,000 in eight to ten years with 20% down. (By that time Christopher should be a partner of the firm.) Housing is expected to increase with inflation. At that time, they will not sell the current house but will rent it.
5. Be free of mortgage indebtedness by the time Christopher is 55 years old.
6. Prepare a proper retirement plan allowing them a "no worry" retirement. They feel that income of $75,000 in today's dollars per year will allow them to keep their fairly high standard of living.
7. Rebuild savings account/emergency fund back to a minimum of $25,000.
8. Save for the twins' future weddings (estimated costs $15,000 each).

ECONOMIC INFORMATION

- Expect inflation to average: 4%
- Expect Tiffany's salary to increase: 5%
- Expect Christopher's salary to increase: 5%
- Marginal tax rate:
  - Federal 15%
  - State 6%
- Mortgage rates:
  - 15-Year Fixed 6.5%
  - 30-Year Fixed 7.0%

Any refinancing will incur 3% of mortgage as a closing cost and will be added to the mortgage.

INSURANCE INFORMATION

Health Insurance

Health insurance is provided for the entire family by Blune & Peeron. The Whites are covered by an HMO. Doctors visits are $10 per visit, while prescriptions are $5 for generic brands and $10 for other brands. There is no co-payment for hospitalization in semi-private accommodations. Private rooms are provided when medically necessary. For emergency treatment, a $50 co-payment is required.

Life Insurance

Christopher has a $50,000 group term life insurance policy through Blune & Peeron. Tiffany has a $20,000 group term policy through Ridgewood Preparatory School. The owners of the policies are Christopher and Tiffany, respectively, with each other as the respective beneficiary.

Disability Insurance

Christopher has disability insurance through the accounting firm. Short-term disability benefits begin for any absence due to accident or illness over six days and will continue for up to six months at 80% of his salary. Long-term disability benefits are available if disability continues over six months. If Christopher is unable to perform the duties of his own current position, the benefits provide him with 60% of his salary while disabled until recovery, death, retirement, or age 65 (whichever occurs first). All disability premiums are paid by Blune and Peeron.

Tiffany currently has no disability insurance.

Malpractice Insurance

Blune and Peeron have malpractice insurance covering all employees.

Homeowners Insurance

The Whites currently have an HO3 policy and Replacement Value on Contents endorsement through Prudential. The policy covers all risk and replacement value. The deductible is $250 with a premium of $533.60 per year.

Automobile Insurance

Christopher and Tiffany have full coverage on both cars, including:

> $100,000 bodily injury for one person
> $300,000 bodily injury for all persons
> $50,000 property damage
> $100,000 uninsured motorist

Deductibles are:

> $500 comprehensive
> $1,000 collision

This insurance includes medical payments, car rentals, and towing.

The cost of the auto insurance is $2,123.50 per year because of a number of speeding tickets Tiffany has received.

INVESTMENT INFORMATION (PROSPECTIVE)

	Expected Return	Beta
Aggressive stocks	13%	1.6
Growth stocks	10%	1.1
S&P 500	9%	1.0
Bonds	7%	0.5
Money Market (Bank)	2%	0.3

The Whites consider themselves to be moderate investors.

INCOME TAX INFORMATION

The Whites are in the 15% marginal tax bracket and pay average Federal taxes of 10%. Their combined marginal tax bracket (Federal and state) is 21%.

RETIREMENT INFORMATION

Christopher and Tiffany would both like to retire when they are 65 and 64, respectively, and they expect to be in retirement for 30 years. They would hope to have a $75,000 per year of pre-tax income in today's dollars during retirement. They do not want to rely on Social Security benefits for their retirement planning. Any money received from Social Security will be considered extra income.

Christopher does not participate in a 401(k) plan available through the accounting firm. In the plan, the firm matches 50 cents for every dollar contributed, up to 6% of his contribution (if he contributes 6% of his salary the company contributes 3%). Christopher may defer a maximum of 16% of his salary.

Tiffany is currently enrolled in a defined contribution plan in which the school contributes 7% of her salary, and she contributes 3%. The plan provides several options for the investment of her controllable funds: Bond Funds, Mutual Stock Funds, or Money Market accounts. She has chosen to invest this contribution in fixed instruments (Bond Fund). The plan has a seven-year graduated vesting schedule, and she has been a participant for five years. The total balance of her account fund is $9,500. Although she has not participated, she also has available a 403(b) supplemental retirement plan in which she may contribute up to 13% of her salary.

GIFTS, ESTATES, TRUSTS, AND WILL INFORMATION

Neither Christopher nor Tiffany has wills. They realize the importance of having a will, however, and would like to have one leaving everything to each other and the children, while at the same time minimizing as much estate and gift tax as possible.

STATEMENT OF CASH FLOWS

Christopher and Tiffany White
Statement of Cash Flows[5]
1998

CASH INFLOWS

Salary - Christopher	$32,500.00	
Salary - Tiffany	18,000.00	
Tutoring - Tiffany[1]	3,600.00	
Interest - Trust	5,000.00	
Savings Account Withdrawal[4]	5,569.80	
Total Inflows		$64,669.80

CASH OUTFLOWS

DC Plan Savings - Tiffany	$ 540.00	
Mortgage Payment (P&I)	9,142.32	
Property Taxes (Residence)	850.00	
FICA	3,863.25	
Federal Withholding	6,822.60	
State Withholding	556.70	
Utilities	2,100.00	
Home Owners Insurance	533.60	
Auto Note	6,374.16	
Auto Expense/Maintenance	2,190.00	
Auto Insurance	2,123.50	
Child Care/Maid[2]	4,800.00	
Education Loans	2,892.60	
Credit Card Interest and Payments[3]	2,170.08	
Dry Cleaning	900.00	
New Clothes	3,600.00	
Food	4,800.00	
Dining Out/Entertainment	4,200.00	
Misc.	600.00	
Child Support (to Amber Dawn)	2,400.00	
Support Payment to Bertha Louisa	1,200.00	
Total Outflows		$62,658.81
Discretionary Cash Flows		$ 2,010.99

Notes to Financial Statements:

1 Tiffany does not report this money to the IRS.

2 The Whites pay the maid in cash and do not report it to the IRS.

3 The Whites pay the minimum monthly interest charge on credit cards.

4 $366 is earned interest.

5 1999 is expected to be similar.

STATEMENT OF FINANCIAL POSITION

Christopher and Tiffany White
Balance Sheet
January 1, 1999

ASSETS:[1]

Checking Account	$ 10,000
Savings Account	13,500
Trust Fund[2]	100,000
Car-Tiffany (1990 BMW 325i)	5,750
Car-Christopher (1997 Nissan Maxima)	16,375
Boat	12,000
Home (appraised 7/1/98)	85,000
401(k) plan-Christopher	0
Pension-Tiffany	9,500
403(b) Tiffany	0
Total Assets	**$252,125**

LIABIILITIES:[3/4]

Credit Card- Christopher (18%)	$ 4,750
Credit Card- Tiffany (23%)	4,920
Credit Card-Joint (16%)	1,200
Car note-Christopher (10%)	18,383
School Loans	17,919
Home Mortgage Balance (10%)	85,561
Total Liabilities	**$132,733**
Net Worth	**$119,392**
Total Liabilities and Net Worth	**$252,125**

Notes To Financial Statements:

1 All assets are stated at fair market value.

2 The Trust Fund is for the kids education; however, Tiffany and Chris receive the interest on the balance of the trust fund until all children reach age of majority. The Trust assets are invested in a CD yielding 5% per year.

3 Liabilities are stated at principal only.

4 % are interest rates on respective indebtedness.

INFORMATION REGARDING ASSETS AND LIABILITIES

Employment

Christopher is currently employed as an upper level senior accountant at Blune & Peeron, earning an annual salary of $32,500. He expects to be promoted to supervisor within two years. Christopher hopes to be a partner in eight years.

Tiffany earns $18,000 a year teaching at Ridgewood Preparatory School. Annual increases range from 3 - 5%. She also earns approximately $3,600 a year tutoring. This money is received in cash. (Although they should, she and Christopher do not report these earnings on their tax returns.) In addition, Tiffany receives $5,000 a year, before taxes, on the interest earned from the childrens' trust fund.

Christopher and Tiffany earn approximately 2% interest on their savings account. This is automatically credited on a quarterly basis to the account; however, this amount is so low that they do not consider it income. This savings account/emergency fund began with an account balance of $25,000 when they were first married. In 1998, they withdrew $366 in interest income and $5,203.80 from the savings account to pay bills.

Home

Christopher and Tiffany purchased a four-bedroom house for $100,000 in a nice, family neighborhood. They were among the first families to purchase a home in this new subdivision. The money from Tiffany's parents was used for the down payment and closing costs. The mortgage payment is $761.86 per month. The interest rate is 10%. The original mortgage was $86,814.57, and they have made 29 payments. Utilities range from $150 - 200 a month.

Although the original value of the house was $100,000, a recent appraisal valued the house at $85,000. The decrease in value did not leave enough equity for the Whites to be approved for a home equity loan. The appraiser explained that the decrease in value was because of the increase of drug traffic in the subdivision. If the Whites wanted to refinance (80% of the fair market value of the home), the 3% closing costs would be added to the mortgage.

Automobiles

In 1997, Christopher purchased a new Nissan Maxima for $25,000. The current value of the car is $16,375, but his loan balance is $18,383.47. His loan was originally for 60 months at 10% interest. He has made 19 monthly payments of $531.18.

Tiffany's prize for winning a State Pageant was a new 1990 BMW 325i. Its current value is $5,750.

Boat

The current value of Christopher's 18 foot Boston Whaler Center Console with a 150 HP Mercury is $12,000. Though Christopher and Tiffany consider this a luxury item, they both know that the sale of the boat would only further erode any relations with Tiffany's parents because they like to use it.

Student Loans

Christopher is essentially a self-made man. He put himself through school with part-time jobs and student loans. He originally borrowed $20,000 to pay for his education through the student loan program. The loan is for 10 years and Christopher is in his second year of payments. The current payment is $241.05 per month.

Credit Cards

Before marriage, Christopher and Tiffany each had their own credit cards almost charged to the limits. After marriage, they applied for a joint credit card and planned to use it for emergency use only. The current interest rates, balances, limits, and annual fees on these cards are as follows:

	Interest	Balance	Limit	Annual Fees
Christopher	18%	$4,750	$5,000	$25
Tiffany	23%	$4,920	$5,000	$25
Joint	16%	$1,200	$5,000	$12

Entertainment

Due to Christopher and Tiffany's hectic work schedules and the three children, they rarely get to spend time alone together. Every Friday night, they go to a modestly priced restaurant for dinner. Sometimes they are joined by some colleagues of Christopher's, and he uses this time to network. The approximate cost of dinner each Friday for Christopher and Tiffany is $60 including tip.

Friday nights is also a night out for the children. Consuela brings the children to Glad Bag for dinner. The approximate cost is $15 for all three children and Consuela.

Education

Due to the quality of the schools in their state, Christopher and Tiffany want John, Ashley, and Allison to go to private schools, but they are concerned about the cost. To assist in defraying the cost of educating the children, it is expected that all three children will attend Ridgewood Preparatory for K – 12th grade. Tiffany's position allows for tuition discounts for teachers as follows:

      50% discount on tuition for students in K - 8th grades
      75% discount on tuition for students in 9 - 12th grades

Current tuition is $3,665 per student. There is no additional "multi-family" discount. Tuition is expected to increase at 5% per year. Each student will begin Kindergarten at age 5.

Christopher and Tiffany would also like to provide financial assistance to their children while they attend college. They have decided to offer each child up to $15,000 (in today's dollars) per year for tuition, room, and board. Any additional funding will be provided by the trust, student loans or part-time employment by the children. Today tuition, fees, etc., average $25,000 for a private university and are expected to increase at a rate of 5% per year. Each child is expected to begin college immediately following graduation from high school at age 18 and attend for four years.

QUESTIONS

1.   List the Whites' financial strengths and weaknesses.

      a)   Strengths:

      b)   Weaknesses:

2.   After reading the case, what additional information would you request from the Whites to complete your data-gathering phase?

3.   Calculate the following financial ratios for the Whites.

$$\frac{\text{Liquid Assets}}{\text{Monthly Expenses}} \quad =$$

$$\frac{\text{Liquid Assets}}{\text{Current Debt Payments}} \quad =$$

$$\frac{\text{Net Worth}}{\text{Total Assets}} \quad =$$

$$\frac{\text{Total Debt}}{\text{Total Assets}} \quad =$$

$$\frac{\text{Total Debt}}{\text{Annual Total Income}} \quad =$$

$$\frac{\text{Annual Housing \& Debt Payments}}{\text{Annual Gross Income}} \quad =$$

$$\frac{\text{Annual Housing Costs}}{\text{Annual Gross Income}} \quad =$$

$$\frac{\text{Investment Assets}}{\text{Annual Gross Income}} \quad =$$

$$\frac{\text{Annual Savings}}{\text{Annual Gross Income}} \quad =$$

4.   Comment on any of the above ratios that you think are important.

5.   Briefly evaluate the Whites' use of debt.

6.   What are all of the tax consequences of the current treatment of the tutoring income?

7.   What, if any, are the tax consequences to the Whites of the multi-family tuition discount the first year when all three children are in school?

8.   Calculate the amount needed today to fund the children's college education (assume an earnings rate of 8%).

9.   Calculate the amount they need to save each month to fund the children's college education. Assume that savings will begin at the end of this month and continue until the youngest child (children) begins college.

10.   Calculate the monthly savings needed for education assuming that savings will continue until the children's college education is completed.

11.   What are the tax consequences that may result from the current treatment of the employment of the housekeeper?

12.   Determine whether the Whites will currently qualify to refinance their home.

13.   (For purposes of this question, ignore if they qualify, but maintain the lender's loan to value requirement.)

Assuming that the Whites decide to use their savings account to refinance their current mortgage, calculate the monthly payment for each of the following:

a)   15-year loan.

b)   30-year loan paid over 30 years.

c)   30-year loan paid over the remaining life of their current mortgage.

14.   Calculate the savings expected from the refinancing for each of the loans mentioned above in Question 13.

15.   Do they qualify for any of the above loans?

16.   If they do not qualify for any of the loans due to the lender counting only $50,500 of income, what actions should they consider to qualify?

17.   Calculate the cash flow needed to meet Bertha Louisa's medical needs. Assume that she lives seven years and that the Whites invest in bonds.

18.   Should the Whites purchase a long-term care insurance policy for Bertha Louisa?

19.   What are the Whites' present insurance needs?

20.   Discuss the Whites' projected estate problems.

21.   What estate planning recommendations would you make to the Whites?

22.   What tax planning recommendations would you make to the Whites?

23.   Calculate the childcare tax credit for the Whites for 1998.

24.   Estimate the tax liability for Federal Income Tax for the Whites. (For purposes of this question only ignore any self-employment tax on the tutoring income.)

25.   What is the present value of child support payments to Amber Dawn to age 18? Assume the Whites invested in the S&P 500.

26.   Would it be beneficial for the Whites to obtain a signed release from Consuela indicating that she does not want witholdings from payments made to her for child care services rendered?

27.   Discuss the trust fund set up for the grandchildren by the Kallenborns. Did the initial funding of this trust create a generation skipping transfer by the Kallenborns?

28.   How much do the Whites need to save on a monthly basis beginning at the end of this month for the down payment in order purchase the five-bedroom home for $175,000? Assume they invest in growth stocks and pay all associated taxes out of their current budget.

29.   Comment on the effectiveness of the child support contractual agreement made between Amber Dawn and Christopher.

30.   Does the trust fund of $100,000 belong in the Whites' statement of financial position?

31. If Tiffany left Ridgewood today, what would be her vested retirement balance?

32. If Tiffany left Ridgewood today, what are her options regarding the balance in her retirement plan?

33. If the Whites had a portfolio with the following asset allocation for retirement, what would be their expected return?

Aggressive stocks	10%
Growth stocks	10%
S&P 500	40%
Bonds	30%
Money Market	10%
	100%

34.   What is the weighted beta of the above portfolio?

35.   Does the above asset allocation match the Whites' financial objectives
        and risk tolerance?

36.   Based on the above portfolio, how much, in today's dollars, would the
        Whites need to fund their retirement?

37.   What are the deficiencies in the current Statement of Financial Position?

38.   Will the homeowners policy provide liability coverage for the boat?

39.   What is the approximate amount of life insurance that Christopher needs to replace all of his income and raises during his work life expectancy assuming an investment rate of return equal to the rate of return associated with growth stocks?

DAMIEN AND SHARON YANDLE

CASE SCENARIO AND QUESTIONS

DAMIEN AND SHARON YANDLE

Table of Contents

DAMIEN AND SHARON YANDLE

Case Scenario and Questions

Damien and Sharon Yandle have come to you, a financial planner, on January 1, 1999 for help in developing a plan to accomplish their financial goals. From your initial meeting together, you have gathered the following information:

PERSONAL BACKGROUND AND INFORMATION

Damien Yandle *(Age 26)*

Damien Yandle is employed as a salesperson for a rapidly growing air conditioning and heating services company. He has been employed with this company for five years. Damien has tremendous potential and has positioned himself for advancement.

Sharon Yandle *(Age 26)*

Sharon Yandle is a Canadian citizen and is employed as an interior design consultant for a home-decorating center. Sharon is studying for her interior design license and plans to become an independent design consultant in three years. Sharon is pregnant with twins. She started maternity leave (paid) for six months beginning late September 1998 and ending two months after the twins are expected to be born.

The Yandles

They met May 3, 1994 while attending a mutual friend's birthday party and were married May 3, 1996. They currently have one child, Kristin, and Sharon is pregnant. The latest ultrasound has determined that she will give birth to twins.

Children

Kristin was born January 1, 1998. The twins are expected to be born in late January 1999. Kristin is perfectly healthy, and there is no history of pregnancy-related complications in either Sharon or Damien's family.

Damien's Parents

Damien's parents, Karen and Marvin, are financially secure and live in California. All of their property is owned as community property. They have known Sharon for a long time and any gift that they make will be to both Damien and Sharon. Karen and Marvin have made no previous taxable gifts.

The Yandles expect Damien's parents either to lend (interest free) or to give them a $30,000 down payment (27% of the purchase price) to purchase a house.

PERSONAL AND FINANCIAL OBJECTIVES

- Damien wants to start his own business in 10 years. In the meantime, he plans to advance in his current job. He wants to open a business similar to his current employer and expects to need $100,000 in today's dollars to start the company.

- The Yandles want to buy a house for approximately $110,000 in a family neighborhood with little or no crime. They expect taxes and homeowner's insurance to average $200 per month combined.

- Sharon would like to pursue an interior design license. Damien wants to sharpen his business skills by attending a local MBA program, which he expects to begin in September 1999. He expects to pay for the program himself. Expected cost is $18,000 ($600 per credit hour in today's dollars).

- They want each of their children to receive a private school education and would like to create a fund for this purpose. Current cost of the desired school is $2,500 per child per year for elementary, $5,000 per year for middle and high school. College tuition is expected to be $8,000 per year (see Economic Information).

- They want to purchase a new car within the next six months ranging between $20,000 and $25,000.

- They would like to buy new furniture for the new house ($8,000 - $10,000 today's dollars).

- They plan to create an Emergency Fund of at least six months salary ($24,000). Currently they only have a small savings balance; therefore, this amount needs to be saved in installments over the next 4 years.
- They plan to retire in 30 years and travel extensively.
- They expect their income to increase by an average of 3.5% over their remaining work life expectancy.
- They both expect to live to age 90.

ECONOMIC INFORMATION

- Expected inflation will average 3.5% (CPI) annually.
- Expected return for the S&P 500 Index is 11%.
- T-bills are currently yielding 5%. The long-term riskless rate is 7% (Treasury Bonds).
- Current mortgage rates are:
    Fixed 15-year: 7.5%
    Fixed 30-year: 8.0%
- Home closing costs are expected to be 3% of any mortgage.
- Savings accounts currently yield 1.5% annually, compounded monthly.
- One-year Certificates of Deposit are currently yielding 5%.
- The unemployment rate is currently 6%.
- College tuition is expected to be $8,000 per year (expected to increase by 5% per year).

INSURANCE INFORMATION

Life Insurance

Insured	Damien
Owner	Damien
Beneficiary	Sharon
Face Amount	$50,000
Cash Value	$0
Type of Policy	Term
Settlement Options	Lump-Sum
Premium	Employer provided

Assumptions for the Purpose of Life Insurance Needs Calculations:

1. The surviving spouse will continue working.
2. Education fund needed is $50,000 in today's dollars.
3. Establish an emergency fund of $24,000 for the survivor.
4. Funeral and debt expenses will be $50,000 (including any probate costs).
5. Survivor income needs are $3,200 per month in today's dollars for a period of 22 years at which time either spouse would be age 48 (this is $1,200 more than is currently earned by either spouse).
6. From age 48 – 67, survivor needs will be $3,000 per month ($1,000 above either spouse's earnings in today's dollar). At age 67, Social Security will provide $750 per month in today's dollars.
7. Retirement needs from age 67 - 90 for the survivor are $2,400 per month in today's dollars.
8. Life insurance proceeds can be invested at the long-term riskless rate.
9. If one of the Yandles dies before retirement, the other will continue working until age 67.
10. Social Security benefits during the dependency period will be $1,125 per month.

Health Insurance

Premium	Employer provided for Damien. Sharon and the children are dependents under Damien's policy
Coverage	Major medical with a $500,000 lifetime limit on 80/20 basis
	Maternity coverage also has 80/20 coinsurance
	Dental coverage is not provided
Deductible	$250 per person (3 person maximum)
Family out-of-pocket limit	$2,500

Disability Insurance

Neither Damien nor Sharon has disability insurance.

Automobile Insurance

Premium	$1,000 total annual premium for both vehicles
Bodily Damage and Property Damage	$10,000/$25,000/$5,000 for each vehicle
Comprehensive	$250 deductible
Collision	$500 deductible

Renter's Insurance

Type	HO 4
Contents Coverage	$35,000
Premium	$600 annually
Deductible	$250
Liability	$100,000
Medical Payments	$1,000 per person

HOMEOWNERS 04 POLICY DECLARATION PAGE

Policy Number: **H04-123-ZA-996**
Policy Period: **12:01 a.m. Central Time at the residence premises**
From: **January 1, 1999** To: **December 31, 1999**

Name insured and mailing address:
Damien and Sharon Yandle
Movin' on Up Apartments
1324 Amway Lane, Apartment 100
Anytown, State 00001

The residence premises covered by this policy is located at the above address unless otherwise indicated.
Same as above.

Coverage is provided where a premium or limit of liability is shown for the coverage.

	Limit of Liability	Premium
SECTION I COVERAGES		
A. Dwelling	**N/A**	**N/A**
B. Other Structures	**N/A**	**N/A**
C. Personal Property	**$35,000**	**$475**
D. Loss of Use	**N/A**	**N/A**
SECTION II COVERAGES		
A. Personal liability: each occurrence	**$100,000**	**$100**
B. Medical payments to others: each occurrence	**$1,000**	**$25**
Total premium for endorsements listed below		
	Policy Total	**$600**

Forms and endorsements made part of this policy:

Number	Edition Date	Title	Premium
Not applicable.			

DEDUCTIBLE - Section I: **$250**
In case of a loss under Section I, we cover only that part of the loss over the deductible stated.
Section II: Other insured locations: **Not applicable.**

[Mortgagee/Lienholder (Name and address)]
Not applicable.

Countersignature of agent/date	Signature/title - company officer

INVESTMENT INFORMATION

Both Damien and Sharon have a high tolerance for risk. They currently have a balance of $3,840 in Damien's 401(k) plan provided by his employer. He is currently deferring 4% of his salary, while the maximum deferral allowed by the plan is 10%. The 401(k) plan offers a variety of mutual funds ranging from aggressive growth stock funds to Treasury money market funds. Damien currently has 100% invested in the Growth Fund.

In 1996, Damien's grandfather gave him ABC stock. The fair market value of the stock at the date of the gift was $6,000. Damien's grandfather originally paid $2,000 for the stock and paid gift tax of $600 on the transfer.

The Yandles required rate of return for investments is 1% below the S&P 500 Index return.

INCOME TAX INFORMATION

Damien and Sharon file a joint tax return. Their total tax rate is 24.65% (Federal income tax average rate is 15%; state income tax amounts to 2% each year; FICA taxes amount to 7.65%).

RETIREMENT INFORMATION

Damien is a participant in his employer's 401(k) plan.
Sharon is planning a $2,000 IRA contribution for 1998.

GIFTS, ESTATES, TRUSTS, AND WILL INFORMATION

Damien and Sharon have simple handwritten wills leaving all probate assets to each other.

LAST WILLS AND TESTAMENTS

Sharon

Last Will and Testament

January 15, 1998

I, Sharon Pieret Yandle, a citizen of Canada domiciled in the United States of America, declare this to be my last will and testament. I revoke all of my prior wills and codicils.

I hereby give all of the property of which I die possessed to Damien Yandle, my husband.

Sharon Pieret Yandle

Damien

Last Will and Testament

January 15, 1998

I, Damien Yandle, a citizen of and domiciled in the United States of America, declare this to be my last will and testament. I revoke all of my prior wills and codicils.

I hereby give all of the property of which I die possessed to Sharon Yandle, my wife.

Damien Yandle

STATEMENT OF CASH FLOWS

Damien and Sharon Yandle
Statement of Cash Flows for 1999
Monthly

CASH INFLOWS:

Salary - Damien[1]	$2,000	
Salary – Sharon[2]	2,000	
Interest Income	15	
Total Inflows[3]		$4,015

CASH OUTFLOWS:

401(k) Deferral Savings	$ 80	
Rent	650	
Groceries	370	
Utilities	70	
Water	25	
Telephone	40	
Auto Fuel	100	
Auto Repair	50	
Cable TV	35	
Child Care	200	
Entertainment	300	
Vacations[4]	375	
Auto Insurance	84	
Life Insurance	0	
Medical Insurance	0	
Renters (HO4) Insurance	50	
State Withholding	80	
Federal Withholding	600	
FICA	306	
Student Loan Damien 1	144	
Student Loan Damien 2	111	
Student Loans Sharon	45	
Credit Card 1 Damien	51	
Gas Card Damien	9	
Credit Card 2 Sharon	42	
Credit Card 3 Sharon	165	
Credit Card 4 Sharon	33	
Total Outflows		$4,015
Discretionary Cash Flow		$ 0

Notes to Financial Statements:
1 $2,000 per month salary = $24,000 per year.
2 $2,000 per month salary = $24,000 per year.
3 Dividend income is reinvested and, therefore, not listed.
4 Vacation = Two vacations costing $4,500 per year; $4,500 ÷ 12 months = $375.

STATEMENT OF FINANCIAL POSITION
Damien and Sharon Yandle
Statement of Financial Position
As of January 1, 1999

ASSETS[1]			LIABILITIES[7] AND NET WORTH		
Cash/Cash Equivalents			**Current Liabilities[8]**		
Checking[2]	$	750	Credit Card 1 (Damien)[9]	$	1,500
Savings[3]		1,000	Credit Card 2 (Sharon)[9]		1,200
Certificate of Deposit[4]		3,000	Credit Card 3 (Sharon)[9]		4,800
EE Savings Bonds[5]		500	Credit Card 4 (Sharon)[9]		950
Total Cash/Cash Equiv.	$	5,250	Gas Card 1 (Damien)[9]		200
			Total Current Liabilities	$	8,650
Invested Assets					
ABC Stock		$10,000	**Long-Term Liabilities[8]**		
Stock Portfolio[6]		22,000	Student Loans[9]		
Damien's 401(k)		3,840	Damien 1		20,000
Total Invested Assets		$35,840	Damien 2		15,000
			Sharon 1		6,000
Personal Use Assets			*Total Long-Term Liabilities*		$41,000
Auto 1		$ 7,500			
Auto 2		4,500	**Total Liabilities**		**$49,650**
Furniture		6,000			
Personal Property		7,000	**Net Worth**		**$16,440**
Total Personal Use Assets		$25,000			
Total Assets		**$66,090**	**Total Liabilities & Net Worth**		**$66,090**

Notes to financial statements:

1. All assets are stated at fair market value.
2. Checking is a non-interest bearing account.
3. Savings Interest of 1.5% annually, compounded monthly.
4. Certificate of Deposit maturing December 1, 1999; Interest of 4.5% annually, compounded monthly.
5. EE Savings Bonds, five bonds with present value of $100 each; interest of 6% annually; Maturity date of 2026.
6. Stock Portfolio in stock account managed by Damien.
7. Liabilities are stated at principal only.
8. All liability payments are as indicated on monthly cash flow statement.
9. The average interest rate for student loans is 10% and for all credit cards is 15%.

INFORMATION REGARDING ASSETS AND LIABILITIES

Detailed Investment Portfolio

Damien's 401(k) plan

Description	Shares	Price/Share	Total Value	97 Returns	98 Returns
Growth Fund	93.00	$41.29	$3,840	13%	7%

Stock Portfolio

Stock	Date Acquired	Cost Basis	Fair Market Value As of 1/1/99	Beta	Current Dividend	Growth of Dividend
A	1/92	$ 300	$ 2,800	1.3	$ 200	3.50%
B	3/94	3,000	700	1.6	33	5.00%
C	5/98	5,000	7,000	1.0	400	4.00%
D	6/98	12,000	2,500	1.1	197	2.00%
E	7/98	9,000	9,000	1.2	500	4.25%
TOTAL		$29,300	$22,000	N/A	$1,330	N/A

Miscellaneous

The Yandles like to take two vacations each year with an average cost of $2,250 per vacation. Damien and Sharon also love to go out with friends or entertain weekly.

QUESTIONS

1.   List the Yandles' financial strengths and weaknesses.

    a.   Strengths:

    b.   Weaknesses:

2.   After reading the case, what additional information would you request from the Yandles to complete your data-gathering phase?

3.   Calculate the following financial ratios for the Yandles.

$$\frac{\text{Liquid Assets}}{\text{Monthly Expenses}} \quad =$$

$$\frac{\text{Liquid Assets}}{\text{Current Debt Payments}} \quad =$$

$$\frac{\text{Net Worth}}{\text{Total Assets}} \quad =$$

$$\frac{\text{Total Debt}}{\text{Total Assets}} \quad =$$

$$\frac{\text{Total Debt}}{\text{Annual Total Income}} \quad =$$

$$\frac{\text{Housing \& Monthly Debt Payments}}{\text{Monthly Gross Income}} \quad =$$

$$\frac{\text{Housing}}{\text{Monthly Gross Income}} \quad =$$

$$\frac{\text{Investment Assets}}{\text{Annual Gross Income}} \quad =$$

$$\frac{\text{Monthly Savings}}{\text{Monthly Gross Income}} \quad =$$

4.   Comment on any of the above ratios that you think are important.

5.   Will the Yandles qualify for either a 15- or 30-year home mortgage loan, assuming that they make a down payment of $30,000 and finance the closing costs in the mortgage?

6.   Assuming that the Yandles qualify for a home mortgage loan, calculate the monthly payment for each of the following:

     a.   15-year loan.

     b.   30-year loan.

7. Assuming they have no current savings set aside, how much should be saved at the end of each month, beginning this month, to be able to acquire Damien's business? Assume they will invest in a no-load S&P 500 index fund and will pay all current taxes out of their regular budget. They will reinvest all earnings in this savings account.

8. How much additional life insurance should be purchased on Damien's life using the needs approach method? (Round to the nearest $100,000.)

9. How much additional life insurance should be purchased on Sharon's life using the needs approach method? (Round to the nearest $25,000.)

10.   How much additional life insurance is needed on Damien's life using a human value approach net of state and Federal income taxes? (Round to nearest $50,000.)   For purposes of this question only, assume Damien's pay increases are 5%.

11.   What is the deduction for Sharon's IRA contribution for 1998?

12.   If Damien was to sell the ABC stock today, what would be the current tax consequences to the Yandles?

13.   Assume Damien has only the following sale transactions in his stock trading account for 1999:

Sold stock	Date	Sales Price/ Net of Commissions
A	August 15, 1999	$ 2,750
B	August 15, 1999	$ 600
C	April 1, 1999	$ 8,000
D	April 1, 1999	$ 3,000
		$14,350 total proceeds

What are the net gains or losses from the above stock transactions during 1999?

14.   If the stock market yields 17%, what is the expected return for the Yandles' stock portfolio under the Capital Asset Pricing Model (CAPM), based on the value as of January 1, 1999?

15.   Based on the constant growth dividend model, which of the stocks (A - E) in the Yandles' stock portfolio is overvalued as of January 1, 1999?

16.   The Yandles want to establish a fund that will provide for each child's college education for a period of four years.   Any post-graduate education will be the responsibility of each individual child. If they can earn an after-tax rate of return equal to the expected return by the S&P 500 Index, how much do they need to save at the end of each year to be able to fund their children's education by the end of 10 years? Assume that the children will all go to a college on their 18th birthday and tuition is paid at the beginning of each year. (Round to the nearest dollar.)

17.   If Damien's parents donate the down payment on the house, what are the tax consequences?

18.   Assuming that Karen and Marvin decide to loan the down payment to Sharon and Damien instead of giving it to them, what are the tax consequences to Karen and Marvin?   The Federal rate for imputed interest is 9%.

19.   Discuss the Yandles' current estate planning deficiencies.

20.   What are the Yandles' present insurance needs?

21.   What are the Yandles' insurance deficiencies?

22.   What estate planning recommendations would you make to the Yandles?

23.   What tax planning recommendations would you make to the Yandles?

USE THE FOLLOWING INFORMATION FOR QUESTIONS 24 THROUGH 30

While on a vacation at Ricky Lake, the Yandles had several unfortunate incidents.

- A large pigeon collided into the windshield of their automobile causing $800 worth of damage while driving to the lake.

- Damien rented a 100 horse power jet ski. While skiing, his wallet was stolen, but he thought he had lost the wallet in the lake so he did not report the loss to the credit card company until he returned home.

- While Damien was jet skiing, Sharon was taken to the emergency room where she gave birth to twins. Mother and children are doing fine.

- While jet skiing, Damien saw the ambulance take Sharon to the hospital. While he was looking at the ambulance, he skied into a boat causing damage to the jet ski, the boat and to Damien. The boat owner had minor medical injuries.

- Upon returning home with the twins and their older child, they discovered that their apartment building had been destroyed by fire.

24.   How much will Damien's insurance company pay to have his windshield repaired from the collision with the pigeon?

25. When Damien received his credit card statements, he discovered that the following amounts had been charged to his credit cards by the thief:

> Credit card 1 $200
>
> Credit card 2 $450
>
> Credit card 3 $35
>
> Credit card 4 $60

How much will Damien be responsible for?

26. The hospital costs for delivery of the twins was $8,000. How much will the insurance company pay?

27. The fire, which destroyed the apartment building, also destroyed all of their personal property. While the depreciated or actual cash value of all their property is $5,000, it would cost the Yandles about $37,000 to replace all of their lost items. How much will the insurance company pay for this loss?

28.   Damien's collision with the boat caused $1,200 of damage to the boat owned by a Mr. George Mitchell. Discuss any coverage provided or issue presented by the HO4 policy.

29.   The boat owner suffered $200 in emergency medical expenses to reset his broken arm caused by the jet ski incident. Discuss any coverage provided by the Yandles' insurance policies.

30.   In the jet ski accident, Damien suffered medical expenses of $1,450. Discuss which of the Yandles' insurance policies, if any, will cover Damien's medical expenses.

31. Which of the following would be appropriate for the Yandles to consider to reduce their current tax liability for 1999?

- Hope credit.
- Education IRA.
- Child tax credit.

THIS PAGE IS INTENTIONALLY LEFT BLANK.

MIKE AND CAROL BRADY

CASE SCENARIO AND QUESTIONS

MIKE AND CAROL BRADY

Table of Contents

MIKE AND CAROL BRADY

Case Scenario and Questions

Mike and Carol have great aspirations for their future. However, they have recently realized that they are not as financially well off as they had thought. As a result, they have come to you for advice on how to solve their current cash flow problems and to help them plan to achieve their financial goals. Assume today is January 1, 1999.

PERSONAL BACKGROUND AND INFORMATION

Mike Brady *(Age 37)*

Mike is a bank vice president. He has been employed there for twelve years and has an annual salary of $70,000.

Carol Brady (Age 37)

Carol is a full-time housewife.

The Bradys

Mike and Carol have been married for eight years. They have two children, and Carol is nine months pregnant. They have always lived in this community and expect to remain indefinitely in their current residence.

Children

Bobby is 6 years old.

Cindy is 3 years old.

The unborn child is due at any time now.

PERSONAL AND FINANCIAL GOALS

- Save for college tuition.
- Pay off all debt by retirement.
- Retire at the age of 62 with 80% of pre-retirement salary at the time of their retirement.
- Prepare proper wills and an estate plan.
- Purchase a new car in two years, twelve years and at retirement. (Total of three cars.)
- Evaluate investment and insurance risk and improve risk management.

ECONOMIC INFORMATION

The Bradys expect medical inflation to be 6% annually and the annual general CPI to average 3% over both the short-term and long-term. The present average interest rate on their credit cards is approximately 16%.

Current mortgage rates are 8.0% for 30 year fixed mortgages and 7.5% for 15 year fixed mortgages. Closing costs will approximate 3.0% of any mortgage refinanced and will be included as part of the refinanced mortgage.

Mike expects salary increases of 4.0% per year for the foreseeable future.

INSURANCE INFORMATION

Health Insurance
The entire family is insured under Mike's company plan (an indemnity plan). There is a $200 family deductible with 80/20 major medical coverage. The plan has a $500,000 lifetime limit for each family member. Mike's employer pays the entire health insurance premium.

Life Insurance

Mike has a term life insurance policy with a face amount of $25,000 provided by his employer. The policy beneficiary is Carol.

Disability Insurance

Mike has a private disability insurance policy covering accidental disability for "own occupation" with a 30-day elimination period. In the event that Mike is disabled as provided under the policy, the benefit is $2,700 per month until age 65. The annual premium is $761 and is paid by Mike.

Homeowners Insurance

The Bradys have a HO3 policy with dwelling extension and replacement cost on contents. There is a $250 deductible. The annual premium is $950.

Automobile Insurance

The Bradys have automobile liability and bodily injury coverage of $100,000/$300,000/$100,000. They have both comprehensive coverage (other than collision) and collision.   The deductibles are $250 (comprehensive) and $500 (collision), respectively. The annual premium is $900.

INVESTMENT INFORMATION

The bank offers a 401(k) plan in which Mike is an active participant. The bank matches contributions dollar for dollar up to 3% of Mike's salary. Mike currently contributes 3% of his salary. Mike's maximum contribution is 16%.

In the 401(k), the Bradys have the opportunity to invest in a Money Market Fund, a Bond Fund, a Growth and Income Fund, and a Small Cap Stock Fund. The Bradys are expecting a retirement period of 30 years. (They expect to live to 92 years of age.)   The Bradys have a moderate investment risk tolerance.

Mike's current 401(k) portfolio is as follows:

Balance				
	Money Market	**Bond**	**Growth and Income**	**Small Cap**	**Total**
Current Balance	$12,000	$12,000	$12,000	$0	$ 36,000*
Current deposits monthly	$ 100	$ 150	$ 100	$0	$350/month includes match
*Loan of $7,000 from 401(k) balance to buy boat (balance is after the loan).				

Expected Returns			
Series	**Geometric Mean**	**Arithmetic Mean**	**Standard Deviation**
Common Stocks	10.4%	12.4%	20.8%
Small Company Stocks	12.1%	17.5%	35.3%
Long-term Corporate Bonds	5.4%	5.7%	8.5%
Long-term Gov't Bonds	4.8%	5.1%	8.6%
Intermediate-term Gov't Bonds	5.1%	5.3%	5.6%
U.S. Treasury Bills	3.7%	3.8%	3.4%
Inflation	3.1%	3.2%	4.7%

INCOME TAX INFORMATION

Mike and Carol tell you that they are barely in the 28% Federal income tax bracket. They pay $820 annually in state and local income taxes.

RETIREMENT INFORMATION

Mike wants to retire at age 62. He wants to retire with income equal to 80% of his pre-retirement income. He expects to receive Social Security benefits of $13,500 (today's dollars) for himself and $6,750 for Carol (today's dollars) at full retirement age 67. They will receive 70% of the full benefit at age 62.

ABBREVIATED FORM-SSA 7004

EXCERPTS FROM SOCIAL SECURITY ADMINISTRATION PERSONAL EARNINGS AND BENEFIT ESTIMATE STATEMENT	

THE FACTS YOU GAVE US

Your Name:	Michael Brady
Your Social Security Number:	990-48-9011
Your Current Age:	37
Current Earnings:	$70,000
Your Estimated Future Average Yearly Earnings:	$70,000
The Age You Plan to Retire:	62
Other Social Security Numbers You've Used	None

YOUR EARNINGS RECORD

	SOCIAL SECURITY				MEDICARE	
YEARS	Maximum Taxable Earnings	Your Taxed Earnings	Subject to FICA	Estimated Taxes You Paid	Your Taxed Earnings	Estimated Taxes You Paid
1985	$39,600	$39,600	$39,600	$2,257	$39,600	$ 534
1986	$42,000	$42,000	$42,000	$2,394	$42,000	$ 609
1987	$43,800	$43,800	$43,800	$2,496	$43,800	$ 635
1988	$45,000	$45,000	$45,000	$2,727	$45,000	$ 652
1989	$48,000	$48,000	$48,000	$2,908	$48,000	$ 696
1990	$51,300	$51,300	$51,300	$3,180	$51,300	$ 743
1991	$53,400	$53,400	$53,400	$3,310	$53,400	$ 774
1992	$55,500	$55,500	$55,500	$3,441	$55,500	$ 805
1993	$57,600	$57,600	$57,600	$3,571	$57,600	$ 835
1994	$60,600	$60,600	$60,600	$3,757	$60,600	$ 879
1995	$62,700	$62,700	$62,700	$3,887	$62,700	$ 909
1996	$64,600	$64,600	$64,600	$4,005	$64,600	$ 937
1997*	$65,400	$65,400	$65,400	$4,055	$70,000	$1,015

ESTIMATED BENEFITS - RETIREMENT

If you retire at 62, your reduced monthly amount in today's dollars will be about	$ 788
Your earliest age at which you can get an unreduced benefit is 67 years of age. We call this your full retirement age. If you wait until that age to get benefits, your monthly amount in today's dollars will be about	$1,125
If you wait until you are 70 to get benefits, your monthly amount will be about	$1,540

*1998 not yet posted

EDUCATION INFORMATION

Bobby is 6 years old and currently attending first grade at a private school. He will attend private school through high school. Mike and Carol have $2,500 in CDs that they contribute to once a year ($500 each year) for Bobby. This account will be used for high school and is in Bobby's name.

Cindy is 3 years old. She will attend private school from pre-kindergarten through high school. Mike and Carol have $1,000 in CDs that they contribute to once a year ($500 each year) for Cindy. This account will be used for high school and is in Cindy's name.

Mike and Carol plan to contribute to CDs for the unborn child's high school education beginning in 2000.

They have set up college funds through CDs. The current balance of the college fund is $15,000 ($7,500 for each child) and the rate of return is 6%. They would also like to be able to send their children to school for five years instead of the traditional four years. The extra year could be used to get a masters or graduate degree. They are currently making no additional contributions to the fund.

The current cost of college (including room, board, tuition, and books) is $15,000 per year per child. They expect their children to start college at the age of 18. The Bradys expect an educational CPI of 5%.

GIFTS, ESTATES, TRUSTS, AND WILL INFORMATION

Mike Brady's will leaves everything to Carol conditioned on a six-month survivorship clause - otherwise equally in separate trusts for Bobby and Cindy.

Carol does not have a will.

STATEMENT OF CASH FLOWS

Mike and Carol Brady
Statement of Cash Flows (Expected)
For the year 1999

CASH INFLOWS

Salary - Mike		$ 70,000
Investment Income		
Interest (Taxable)	$ 900	
Dividends	150	
Total investment income		$ 1,050
Total Cash Inflows		$ 71,050

CASH OUTFLOWS

Planned Savings		
Reinvestment Interest/dividends	$ 1,050	
401(k)	2,100	
High School Fund	1,000	
Total Savings		$ 4,150
Ordinary Living Expenses		
Food	$ 6,000	
Clothing	3,600	
Babysitters	600	
Entertainment	1,814	
Utilities	3,600	
Auto Maintenance	2,000	
Church	3,500	
Total Ord. Living Expenses		$ 21,114
Other Payments		
401(k) Repayment	$ 1,703	
Credit Card Payments	960	
Mortgage Payment	21,954	
Boat Loan	3,040	
Total Payments		$ 27,657
Insurance Premiums		
Automobile	$ 900	
Disability	761	
Homeowners	950	
Total Insurance Premiums		$ 2,611
Tuition and Education Expenses		$ 1,000
Taxes		
Federal Income Tax (W/H)	$ 7,500	
State (and City) Income Tax	820	
FICA	5,355	
Property Tax for Real Estate (Principal Residence)	1,000	
Total Taxes		$ 14,675
Total Cash Outflows		$ 71,207
Discretionary Cash Flow (Deficit)		$ (157)

STATEMENT OF FINANCIAL POSITION

Mike and Carol Brady
Balance Sheet as of January 1, 1999

ASSETS:[1]

Liquid Assets		
Checking Account	$ 1,500	
Savings Account	1,000	
Total Liquid Assets		$ 2,500
Investments		
ABC Stock[2]	$ 13,000	
Certificates of Deposit (college fund)	15,000	
401(k) Plan	36,000	
Total Investments		$ 64,000
Personal Real Estate-Residence		$250,000
Other Personal Assets		
Automobiles	$ 15,000	
Boat	20,000	
Jewelry	13,500	
Furniture/Household	60,000	
Total Other Per. Assets		$108,500
TOTAL ASSETS		$425,000

LIABILITIES[3] AND NET WORTH:

Current Liabilities-Credit Cards		$ 4,000
Long-term Liabilities		
Mortgage on Residence	$197,888	
Boat Loan	13,559	
Total Long-term Liabilities		$211,447
Total Liabilities		$215,447
Brady Family Net Worth		$209,553
TOTAL LIABILITIES AND NET WORTH		$425,000

Notes to Financial Statements:

1 Assets are stated at fair market value.

2 The ABC stock was inherited from Carol's aunt on November 15, 1998 who originally paid $20,000 on October 31, 1998 for it. The fair market value at the aunt's death was $12,000.

3 Liabilities are stated at principal only.

INFORMATION REGARDING ASSETS AND LIABILITIES

Home

The Bradys own a home in the city that was purchased two years ago for $250,000. The value of the house has appreciated; however, because the Bradys paid more than the value of the home at the time of the sale, the current value is equal to the price paid.   At the time of purchase, a $50,000 down payment was made, and the remaining amount was financed.   They own two automobiles, which have values of $10,000 and $5,000, respectively.

Boat

The Bradys own a 100 horsepower speedboat valued at $20,000.

Debt

Asset	Acquired	Price	Debt/Initial Mortgage	Interest Rate	Term	Current Monthly Payment	Balance of Debt
Residence	01/01/97	$250,000	$200,000.00	10.5	30 yr.	$1,829.48	$197,887.67
Boat	05/01/98	$ 20,000	$ 14,350.75	12.0	7 yr.	$ 253.33	$ 13,558.54
Credit card				16.0		$ *80.00	$ 4,000.00
401(k)	05/01/98		$ 7,000.00	8.0	5 yr.	$ 141.93	$ 6,319.64

*The minimum payment, they also charge about $100 per month on the credit cards.

QUESTIONS

1.   List the Bradys' financial strengths and weaknesses.

    a.   Strengths:

    b.   Weaknesses:

2.   After reading the case, what additional information would you request from the Bradys to complete your data-gathering phase?

3.   Calculate the following financial ratios for the Bradys.

$$\frac{\text{Liquid Assets}}{\text{Current Debt Payments}} \quad =$$

$$\frac{\text{Net Worth}}{\text{Total Assets}} \quad =$$

$$\frac{\text{Total Debt}}{\text{Annual Gross Income}} \quad =$$

$$\frac{\text{Housing}}{\text{Monthly Gross Income}} \quad =$$

$$\frac{\text{Housing \& Monthly Debt Payments}}{\text{Monthly Gross Income}} \quad =$$

$$\frac{\text{Investment Assets}}{\text{Annual Gross Income}} \quad =$$

$$\frac{\text{Monthly Savings}}{\text{Monthly Gross Income}} \quad =$$

4.   Comment on any of the ratios from the previous problem that you think
        are important.

5.   Can the Bradys qualify to refinance their home for the following:
        (Do not include 401(k) payment.)

        a.   15-year loan.

        b.   30-year loan paid over 30 years.

6.   Should they refinance their home?

7.   How much will be the monthly savings from refinancing over the term of the loan?

8.   Is the term of the refinanced loan the appropriate term over which to evaluate the savings from refinancing?

9.   Calculate the educational funding needs. (Assume the first payment will be made in one year.)

     a.   To starting date of college (determined separately for Bobby and Cindy only).

     b.   Through the end of college for Cindy.

     c.   By age 45 for Cindy.

10. Are they currently saving enough in CD's to provide for the educational needs?

11. Are CD's the appropriate vehicle for educational funding?

12. Should the Bradys put the CD or any investment for college education in the child's name? In a trust? If so, which one would be more beneficial?

13.   Calculate Mike and Carol's approximate Federal tax liability for 1999. What is the significance of your calculation? Assume no refinancing.

14.   If they refinance and taxes are properly withheld, what does their discretionary cash flow look like?

15.   If the Bradys put all savings from refinancing and withholding into the 401(k) including any tax savings on the deposits, how much would they be saving annually in the 401(k)?

16.   Is the boat covered for liability under the Bradys' homeowners policy?

17.   What are Mike's current life insurance needs? Assume for this question that any last illness, funeral, and administrative expenses will be $25,000.

18.   Discuss the life insurance needs for Carol.

19.   What are the deficiencies of Mike's disability insurance coverage?

20.   What are the risks that the Bradys may face with respect to their health coverage?

21.   Discuss any other insurance deficiencies that the Bradys have.

22. Calculate capital needs for retirement at age 62 on an annuity basis assuming an investment rate of return of 10% pre-tax.

23. Calculate capital needs for retirement on a capital preservation basis.

24. Calculate capital needs for retirement on a purchasing power preservation basis.

25.   How much should they save at the end of each month to meet their retirement objectives? Assume an investment return of 10% annually.

26.   Approximately how much will Mike and Carol receive in Social Security benefits at age 62 in today's dollars?

27.   Should Mike take Social Security at age 62 or age 67?

28. What is the maximum that participants may borrow from a 401(k) plan?

29. What is the payback period for loans from the 401(k) plan?

30. What happens with any loan balance from the 401(k) plan if Mike quits his job?

31.   What is the effect of the six-month survivorship clause in Mike's current will?

32.   What will provisions should the Bradys include in their revised wills?

33.   Discuss the need for a durable power of attorney and explain the purpose of such a document.

34.   What is the Bradys' tax basis in the ABC stock?

35.   What is the tax consequence of selling the ABC stock for the current fair market value?

36.   How could the Bradys update their will and be sure that all children born and unborn would be included in the will?

THIS PAGE IS INTENTIONALLY LEFT BLANK.

ALEX AND SARA ALBRITE

CASE SCENARIO AND QUESTIONS

ALEX AND SARA ALBRITE

Table of Contents

ALEX AND SARA ALBRITE

Case Scenario and Questions

Alex and Sara Albrite have come to you, a financial planner, for help in developing a plan to accomplish their financial goals. From your initial meeting, you have gathered the following information. Assume today is January 1, 1999.

PERSONAL BACKGROUND AND INFORMATION

Alex Albrite (Age 37)

Alex is the owner/manager of a bar named Marlo's. Marlo's is a small, neighborhood bar that is open only at nights and has five part-time employees (<1,000 hours each). Alex inherited the bar four years ago from his Uncle Marlo. Alex attended Arizona State University and received a BBA in Management. He became employed by Texas Energy Resources Inc., an oil and gas exploration company based in Austin, Texas, after graduation. The company paid for Alex to attend graduate school at the University of Texas-Austin. He went part-time at night and earned his MBA. He was the Human Resource Manager and had a salary of $78,500 when he inherited the bar in December of 1994. Because of the volatility in the oil and gas industry, Alex felt that Marlo's afforded him a more stable working environment and a chance for self-employment. In January of 1995, he decided to leave Texas Energy Resources, Inc. and dedicate all of his efforts to Marlo's.

Sara Albrite (Age 37)

Sara is a loan officer at Wood National Bank. She has been employed by Wood for eight years. She attended Texas Christian University and received her BBA in Finance. She also attended the University of Texas-Austin and earned her MBA. They resided in an apartment in Austin until 1993 when Alex was transferred to San Antonio by Texas Energy Resources, Inc. Sara transferred to San Antonio and maintained her position at the Wood National Bank in San Antonio.

The Albrites

Alex and Sara have been married for 11 years. They both plan to retire in 25 years. They own a three bedroom house with a pool, two cars, and a bar (Marlo's) in San Antonio, Texas. They have three children and do not plan on having any more children.

Sebastian Albrite (Age 10)

Sebastian attends Davy Crockett Grammar School (the local public school) and is in the fourth grade.

Sandy Albrite (Age 5)

Sandy also attends Davy Crockett Grammar School (the local public school) and is in kindergarten. Sandy spends the afternoon at Alamo Day Care.

April Albrite (Age 2)

April attends Alamo Day Care Center for nine hours a day, Monday through Friday.

Gerdi Albrite (Age 62)

Alex's mother, Gerdi was widowed four years ago when her husband was age 60. Her only income is $600 a month from Social Security and $500 a month from Alex and Sara. She does not spend the $600 from Social Security; she simply puts it in her money market account. She lives about 100 miles from Alex and Sara.

Maria Rodriguez (Age 70)

Sara's mother, Maria, is a life-long resident and citizen of Columbia and is fully supported by Alex and Sara. It costs Alex and Sara $300 a month to support Maria.

PERSONAL AND FINANCIAL GOALS

The Albrites have the following financial objectives in order of priority:

1. Provide a standard of living after retirement of 80% of their pre-retirement earnings.

2. Accumulate sufficient assets to send the children to a state university away from home yet in the state of Texas.

3. Minimize their current income tax liability.

4. Expand Marlo's to include a daytime grill within the next five years.

5. Be mortgage free at retirement.

6. Develop an estate plan to minimize estate tax liabilities.

ECONOMIC INFORMATION

- The Albrites expect inflation to average 3% annually, both currently and for the long-term.

- The Albrites expect Sara's salary to increase 5% annually, both currently and long-term.

- Current mortgage rates are 7.5% for 15 years and 8.0% for 30 years. Closing costs of 3% will be added to any refinanced loan.

INSURANCE INFORMATION

Life Insurance

	Policy 1	Policy 2
Insured	Sara	Alex
Policy Through	Employer	State Farm
Face Amount	$50,000	$150,000
Type	Term(Group)	Whole
Cash Value	$0	$21,250*
Annual Premium	$102 (Employer Paid)	$2,361
Beneficiary	Alex	Sara
Contingent Beneficiary	3 children	none
Policy Owner	Sara	Alex**
Settlement Options	None	Life Annuity

* Alex's after tax savings rate is 6%. Cash value at January 1, 1998 was $20,900, and the 1998 dividend was $100.

** Community property.

Sara also has an accidental death and dismemberment policy through Sara's employer. She is covered for $100,000 under this policy. She pays a premium of $68 per year for this coverage.

Health Insurance

All family members are covered by Sara's employer under a group health plan with an annual family deductible of $400. After the deductible is met, the plan pays 100% of the first $2,000 of covered hospital charges for each hospital stay and 80% thereafter. There is a stop-loss maximum of $2,000 including the deductible. The plan will then pay 100% of any other covered expenses, as long as they are reasonable and customary, and incurred that year - no matter how high the amount.

Dental Insurance

The Albrites have dental insurance. The premium is $216 annually.

Disability Insurance

Alex has a personal disability policy with an "own occupation" definition that provides a benefit of $2,000 per month disability income and has a 14-day elimination period. The policy was purchased from a local insurance company. This policy covers both accidents and sickness and has a benefit period of five years. His annual premium is $608.

Sara has an "own occupation" definition that provides a benefit of 65% of gross pay and has a 90-day elimination period policy. The policy is provided through her employer. The policy covers both accidents and sickness to age 65. The annual premium is $460, and the employer and Sara each pay half.

Homeowner's Insurance

The Albrites have a HO-3 Policy (replacement value) with a $250 deductible and a dwelling value of $97,000 purchased through State Farm Insurance Co. (Premium is $739 per year.) $100,000 liability per person.

Automobile Insurance

Both Cars	
Type	Personal Auto Policy (PAP)
Liability	$100,000/$300,000
Medical Payments	$5,000 per person/accident
Physical Damage, own car	Actual cash value
Uninsured Motorist	$50,000/accident
Collision Deductible	$100
Comprehensive Deductible	$250
Premium (Per Year)	$1,080

INVESTMENT DATA

The Albrites tolerance for investment risk on a scale of 1 to 10 (1 being the most risk averse) is a 7. They expect to be more conservative as they get closer to retirement.

INCOME TAX INFORMATION

Their marginal income tax rate is currently 28% for Federal income taxes, and there are no state income taxes in Texas.

RETIREMENT INFORMATION

The Albrites plan to retire in 25 years when they are 62 years old. They would like to have a standard of living equal to 80% of their pre-retirement income. At or before retirement, the Albrites plan to sell the bar and travel. They expect to be in retirement for 28 years.

Sara has a 401(k) plan through Wood National Bank. Wood matches $1 for every $4 contributed by Sara up to an employer maximum contribution of 2% of salary. The maximum employee contribution without regard to the match is 10% of her salary. She has been contributing 5% of her salary since she began working there in 1990. Her 401(k) has averaged an annual return of 7% over the past eight years. Her estate is currently designated as the beneficiary.

Alex has an IRA account through his banker. He opened the account 10 years ago and has been contributing $2,000 each year. He has averaged a 6% annual return over the past 10 years. He always contributes on January 1st of the year in question. His estate is the beneficiary of the IRA.

Alex expects to collect $13,500 in Social Security benefits at age 66 or 70% of full retirement benefits at age 62 (in today's dollars). Sara expects to collect $9,000 in Social Security benefits at age 66 and 70% at age 62 (in today's dollars). They expect to begin receiving Social Security benefits as soon as they retire.

GIFTS, ESTATES, TRUSTS, AND WILL INFORMATION

The Albrites have simple wills leaving all probate assets to each other.

STATEMENT OF CASH FLOWS
Alex and Sara Albrite
For the Year Ended December 31, 1998 (Annual Basis)

INFLOWS

Alex's Net Income from the Bar (Schedule C)	$64,000	
Sara's Salary	57,200	
Dividend Income	777	
Checking Interest Income	130	
Savings Interest Income	400	
Certificate of Deposit	275	
Total Inflows		$122,782

OUTFLOWS

Planned Savings

401(k) 5% for Sara	$ 2,860	
IRA	2,000	
Total Planned Savings		$ 4,860

Ordinary Living Expenses

Mortgage (P&I)	$10,267	
Homeowner's Insurance Premium	739	
Church Donations-Cash	5,200	
Lease on Honda	3,588	
P&I on Cherokee	7,800	
Gas/Oil/Maintenance	2,000	
Auto Insurance payments (Both cars)	1,080	
Credit Card Payments	6,200	
Taxes on income	41,018	
Property taxes on residence	2,657	
Utilities	1,200	
Telephone	600	
Life Insurance Premiums (Alex)	2,361	
Accidental Death & Dismemberment	68	
Support for Gerdi and Maria	9,600	
Health	2,592	
Dental Insurance	216	
Child Care (paid to Alamo)	4,500	
Disability Premium (Both)	838	
Vacation expense	4,000	
Entertainment expense	3,250	
Food	3,250	
Clothing	3,000	
Total Ordinary Living Expenses		$116,024
Total Outflows		$120,884
Discretionary Funds Available		$ 1,898

NOTES ON TAXES:

FICA-Alex (15.3% x $64,000 x .9235)[1]	$ 9,043	
FICA-Sara (7.65% x $57,200)	4,375	
Estimated Payments (Alex)	12,600	
Federal withholding Sara	15,000	
Total Income Taxes	$41,018	

1 The self-employment FICA is calculated using Schedule SE of Form 1040. Although not done in all of the cases in this book, this method is the proper method to calculate self-employment tax.

STATEMENT OF FINANCIAL POSITION

Alex and Sara Albrite
December 31, 1998

ASSETS[1]

Cash/Cash Equivalents

Checking Account (2.5%)	CP	$	5,200
Savings Account (3.25%)[2]	CP		12,300
Total Cash/Cash Equivalents		$	7,500

Invested Assets

Certificate of Deposit (5.5%, 2 yrs., mat. 12/31/00)	CP	$	5,000
Savings Bonds (zero coupon EE bonds)	CP		4,000
Mutual Funds	CP		18,800
Stocks	CP		13,600
401(k) Plan (Sara)	CP		31,331
IRA (Alex)	CP		27,942
Proprietorship in bar	CP		138,000
Rental Property	W		84,000
Cash value life insurance	CP		21,250
Total Investments			$343,923

Personal Use Assets

House (Land is $20,000)	CP		$125,000
Jewelry (1 diamond)	CP		8,000
1995 Jeep Grand Cherokee	CP		24,000
Baseball Card Collection	H		2,400
Total Personal Use			$159,400
Total Assets			**$520,823**

LIABILITIES AND NET WORTH[3]

Current Liabilities

Credit card balances (14.7%)	$	8,200
Car loan (Jeep Cherokee)		11,000
Total Current Liabilities	$	19,200

Long-Term Liabilities

Home Mortgage (9.25% for 30 years)	$	98,836
Total Long-Term Liabilities	$	98,836

TOTAL LIABILITIES	$118,036
NET WORTH	$402,787
Total Liabilities and Net Worth	**$520,823**

Notes to Financial Statements:
1 Assets are stated at fair market value.
2 The savings account is currently serving as their emergency fund.
3 Liabilities are stated at principal only and are all community obligations.

General Note: The bracketed numbers indicate the interest rate being charged on the debt.

CP = Community property
H = Husband's separate property
W = Wife's separate property

INFORMATION REGARDING ASSETS AND LIABILITIES

Marlo's

Marlo's is located one block off of the local college campus and has been in business for 32 years.   Marlo had a taxable basis in the bar of $10,000 at his death. The fair market value at the time of Marlo's death was $40,000. In 1997, Alex executed a legal document making Marlo's community property with Sara.

Alex completely refurbished the bar in 1995 at a cost of $30,000. The building and property is currently valued at $78,000.   Property taxes are high in this district; they are currently $2,278 (2.92 per hundred). The bar could be sold at fair market value of $138,000 and is increasing at 3.5% per year. The bar's net income and cash flows for the last three years was $64,000 (1998), $59,600 (1997), and $57,500 (1996).

They also expect Alex's net income and cash flows from Marlo's to increase at 3.5% annually, both currently and over the long run.

Personal Residence

The Albrites purchased their home and financed the mortgage over 30 years at 9.25%. The house is a two-story, three bedroom, brick house. It has a pool and a monitored burglar alarm.

Rental Property

The rental property, which is valued at $84,000, is located in Austin, Texas and consists of a small strip shopping center. It is in a poor location and is currently a break-even proposition with income equaling expenses. The property was acquired from Sara's Aunt Grace in 1995 as a gift. Grace had a basis in the property of $20,000 and paid gift tax on the transfer of $24,000. At the time of the gift, the property had a fair market value of $60,000. Grace died recently and at the time of her death the property was valued at $84,000.

Prior to Grace's death, Sara and Alex would never dispose of the rental property for fear of offending Grace. However, they want to buy a strip shopping center in San Antonio at a cost of $100,000 using a small mortgage of $16,000. There is a tenant in the Austin property who would buy the rental property for the fair market value of $84,000.

Mutual Funds

	FMV	Beta	Expected Return
Balanced Fund	$ 5,600	0.65	8.5%
Growth Fund	2,400	1.24	12.4%
Bond fund	10,800	0.55	6.5%
Total	$18,800		

5, 6, 9, 21

QUESTIONS

1.   List the Albrites' financial strengths and weaknesses.

      a.   Strengths:

      b.   Weaknesses:

2.   After reading the case, what additional information would you request from the Albrites to complete your data-gathering phase?

3.   Calculate the following financial ratios for the Albrites:

$$\frac{\text{Liquid Assets}}{\text{Monthly Expenses}} =$$

$$\frac{\text{Liquid Assets}}{\text{Current Debt Payments}} =$$

$$\frac{\text{Net Worth}}{\text{Total Assets}} =$$

$$\frac{\text{Total Debt}}{\text{Total Assets}} =$$

$$\frac{\text{Total Debt}}{\text{Annual Total Income}} =$$

$$\frac{\text{Housing \& Monthly Debt Payments}}{\text{Monthly Gross Income}} =$$

$$\frac{\text{Housing Costs}}{\text{Monthly Gross Income}} =$$

$$\frac{\text{Investment Assets}}{\text{Annual Gross Income}} =$$

$$\frac{\text{Monthly Savings}}{\text{Monthly Gross Income}} =$$

4.   Comment on any of the above ratios that you think are important.

5.   Assuming the Albrites have always made their mortgage payments exactly as agreed, how much was their original mortgage?

6.   How many payments have they made on the mortgage loan (assume that they paid as agreed)?

7.   How much qualified residence interest can they deduct on their income
        tax return for 1998?

8.   Do the Albrites qualify to refinance their house?

9.   If they refinance, how much will they save over the life of the loan for a
        15- or 30-year loan? Which loan should they select?

10.   What other method might they consider to save on the repayment of the mortgage?

11.   Is Gerdi a dependent of the Albrites for income tax purposes in 1998? Explain why.

12.   Is Maria Rodriquez a dependent of the Albrites for income tax purposes in 1998? Explain why.

13.   How much of a child care credit, if any, can the Albrites take in 1998?

14.   Can Alex take a deductible IRA as an alternative to or as an addition to any qualified plan he may implement?

15.   Estimate the Albrites' Federal income tax liability for 1998.

16.   What kinds of qualified plans can Alex adopt for Marlo's, since it is a sole proprietorship?

17.   What qualified plan type should Alex adopt if he wishes to (1) maximize his contributions and (2) minimize his cash flow commitment?

18.   What is the maximum contribution Alex can make to a qualified defined contribution plan in the current year?

19.   What would be the impact on the Albrites' tax liability for 1998 if Alex were to establish a Keogh and maximize his contributions?

20.   What is the projected value of Marlo's at Alex's expected retirement date using the current Balance Sheet valuation?

21.   Calculate the Albrites' capital needed at retirement. Assume an earnings rate of 11%.

22.   Calculate the capital needed at retirement for the Albrites using the Annuity Approach.

23.   Calculate the capital needed at retirement for the Albrites using the Capital Preservation Approach.

24.   Calculate the capital needed at retirement for the Albrites using the Purchasing Power Preservation Approach.

25.   Explain the differences between the Capital Preservation model and the Purchasing Power Preservation model.

26.   Can Sara make an in-service withdrawal from her 401(k) if Marlo's needs cash flow?

27.   Can Sara's 401(k) plan have a loan provision?

28.   Gerdi is considering going back to work and wants to know how much she can earn before she will lose any Social Security benefits.   How much will she have to make to lose all benefits?

29.   What are the income tax consequences of any disability benefits received by Alex?

30.   What are the income tax consequences of disability benefits received by Sara?

31.   Discuss the strengths and weaknesses of disability benefits for Alex and Sara.

32.   Is the life insurance amount adequate for Alex and Sara?

33.   Is the health care insurance coverage adequate?

34.   Is the homeowners insurance coverage appropriate?

35.   Analyze the Albrites' liability insurance coverage.

36.   Should Alex replace his whole life policy? Use the Belth Model.

37.   What estate deficiencies do the Albrites have?

38.   What is the total of all the assets that will be included in Alex's probate estate if he were to die today?

39.   What could be done to reduce Alex's probate estate?

40.   Calculate the value of Alex's gross estate assuming he died today.

41.   What is Sara's adjusted taxable basis in the Austin rental property?

42.   What are the tax consequences of a sale of the Austin rental property?

43.   If instead of a sale of the Austin property, Sara uses a tax-free exchange to acquire the San Antonio shopping center, what is her recognized gain or loss from the Austin property and her basis in the new property?

44.   What is Alex and Sara's adjusted taxable basis in Marlo's?

45.   If Alex were to die today and Sara inherited and sold Marlo's for the current Balance Sheet value, what would be her income adjusted basis at the time of the sale?

THIS PAGE IS INTENTIONALLY LEFT BLANK.

TOM AND SUE SMITH

CASE SCENARIO AND QUESTIONS

TOM AND SUE SMITH

Table of Contents

TOM AND SUE SMITH

Case Scenario and Questions

Today is January 1, 1999. Tom and Sue Smith have come to you, a financial planner, for help in developing a plan to accomplish their financial goals. From your initial meeting together, you have gathered the following information:

PERSONAL BACKGROUND AND INFORMATION

Tom Smith *(Age 47)*

Tom Smith is an executive in the ABC Company, a closely held corporation. His salary is $100,000, and he expects increases of 5% per year.

Sue Smith *(Age 50)*

Sue Smith is Tom's administrative assistant. Her present salary is $24,000. She expects raises of 5% per year.

This is a second marriage for Sue. Her first husband, Jerry, was killed in January 1994. Sue was the beneficiary of Jerry's $250,000 life insurance policy with which she created her investment portfolio.

Sue is very vigorous, and women on her family's side have continued to have children into their fifties.

The Smiths

Tom and Sue have been married for three years. They do not reside in a community property state.

The Children

Sue has two children from her first marriage, Jerry, Jr. (age 16) and Christopher (age 12). Tom and Sue have one daughter, Kelsey, who is now 2 years old. All of the children live with them. They may or may not consider having additional children. The children are cared for during the day by their paternal grandmother who lives next door.

When they were first married, Tom wanted to adopt Jerry, Jr. and Christopher, but the children did not agree. Since then, Tom and the two boys have been in continual conflict. As a result, Sue expects to use her investment portfolio to pay for the boys' education, without any assistance from Tom.

PERSONAL AND FINANCIAL GOALS

1. The Smiths want to aggressively begin planning for their children's college education. They plan for each child to attend a private institution for five years beginning at age 18 with a cost of $25,000 a year per child (today's cost). The expected educational inflation rate is 6%.
2. Tom and Sue expect to need 80% of their pre-retirement income during retirement. Sue would like to retire at age 65 and Tom at age 62. They expect the retirement period to be 30 years.
3. Tom wants to review both his and Sue's life insurance needs and have wills drafted for both of them.
4. They would like to minimize any estate tax liability.
5. Tom and Sue plan to travel extensively during retirement.
6. They want to be free of all debt by the time they retire.

ECONOMIC INFORMATION

- Inflation has averaged 4% over the last 20 years.
- Inflation is expected to be 3.5% in the future.

(Assumed)
Treasury Yield Curve

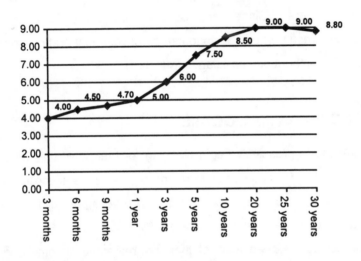

Current Yields for Treasury Securities

3 months	6 months	9 months	1 year	3 years	5 years	10 years	20 years	25 years	30 years
4.0%	4.5%	4.7%	5.0%	6.0%	7.5%	8.5%	9.0%	9.0%	8.8%

Current Mortgage Rates

- 8.75% for 30-year loans
- 8.25% for 15-year loans

Refinancing will cost 3% of any mortgage as closing costs and will be included in any new mortgage.

Economic Outlook-Investments

	Expected returns (pre-tax)	Expected Standard Deviation
Aggressive stocks	18%	15%
Growth stocks	14%	10%
S&P 500	11%	8%
Bonds	8%	3%
Insurance contracts	6%	2%
Money markets	5%	1%
T-bills	4%	1%

INSURANCE INFORMATION

Life Insurance

	Policy A	Policy B	Policy C	Policy D
Insured	Tom	Tom	Sue	Sue
Owner	Tom	Tom	Sue	Sue
Beneficiary	Tom's mother	Estate of Tom	Jerry, Jr. & Christopher	Jerry, Jr. & Christopher
Original Amount	$200,000	$100,000	$48,000	$50,000
Type	Group Term	Term 30 year declining balance	Group Term	Whole Life
Cash Value	$0	$0	$0	$0
Settlement Options	N/A	N/A	N/A	N/A
Annual Premium	$250	$100	$60	$420
Who Pays Premium	Employer	Tom	Employer	Sue
Date Purchased	Annually	1977	Annually	1994
Current Coverage	$200,000	$75,000	$48,000	$50,000

Health Insurance

The entire family is covered under the ABC health plan. The Smiths currently pay $200 per month for the employer provided indemnity plan. The deductible is $200 per person up to three persons. There is a stop loss of $2,000 per year and an 80/20 major medical coinsurance provision.

Disability Insurance

Tom has a personally owned disability insurance policy that covers accident and sickness and has an "own occupation" definition with a 180-day elimination period. The policy pays benefits of 60% of current gross pay (payable until age 65).

Homeowners Insurance

	HO2 Policy
Dwelling	$150,000
Other Structure	$ 15,000
Personal Property	$ 75,000
Loss of Use*	$ 30,000 (20% of dwelling)

*There is no rider for replacement value on personal property.

There is an endorsement for furs and jewelry (premium $30 annually).

SCHEDULED PERSONAL PROPERTY ENDORSEMENT

THIS ENDORSEMENT CHANGES THE POLICY. PLEASE READ CAREFULLY.

For an additional premium, we cover the classes of personal property indicated by an amount of insurance. This coverage is subject to the DEFINITION, SECTION 1 - CONDITIONS, SECTIONS I AND II - CONDITIONS and all provisions of this endorsement. The Section I deductible as shown on the Declarations does not apply to this coverage.

Class of Personal Property	Amount of Insurance	Premium
1. **Jewelry**, as scheduled.	$*10,000	$*30
2. **Furs** and garments trimmed with fur or consisting principally of fur, as scheduled.	Same as 1	
3. **Cameras**, projection machines, films and related articles of equipment, as listed.	5,000	30
4. **Musical Instruments** and related articles of equipment, as listed. You agree not to perform with these instruments for pay unless specifically provided under this policy.		
5. **Silverware**, silver-plated ware, goldware, gold-plated ware and pewterware, but excluding pens, pencils, flasks, smoking implementings or jewelry.		
6. **Golfer's equipment** meaning golf clubs, golf clothing and golf equipment.		
7a. **Fine Arts**, as scheduled. This premium is based on your statement that the property insured is located at the following address. At At	Total Fine Arts Amount $	
7b. For an additional premium, paragraph 5.b. under Perils Insured Against is deleted only for the articles marked with a double asterisk (**) in the schedule below.	Amount of 7.b. only $	
8. **Postage Stamps**		
9. **Rare and Current Coins**		

SCHEDULE*		
Article	**Description**	**Amount of Insurance**
Diamond Bracelet	12 pure 1/3k diamonds, 14k white gold setting	$3,000
Diamond Necklace	18" 14k gold chain, pure 2k diamond pendant	$7,000
T-Max 90	35 mm body	$ 500
300Z lens		$3,000
Hasenbladt	camera body + 2 lens	$1,500

THE AMOUNTS SHOWN FOR EACH ITEM IN THE SCHEDULE ARE LIMITED BY CONDITION 2. LOSS SETTLEMENT ON PAGE 3 OF THIS ENDORSEMENT

* Entries may be left blank if shown elsewhere in this policy for this coverage

HO 04 61 04 91

Page 1 of 3

SPECIAL LIMITS ON PERSONAL PROPERTY

Property Description	Special Limits
Money, bank notes, bullion, gold other than goldware, silver other than silverware, platinum, coins, and medals	$200
Securities, accounts, deeds, evidences of debt, letters of credit, notes other than bank notes, manuscripts, personal records, passports, tickets, and stamps	$1,000 regardless of whether printed on paper or stored on computer disks
Watercraft - including outboard motors, furnishings, equipment, and trailers	$1,000
Any trailer not used with watercraft, such as a utility or camping trailer	$1,000
Jewelry, watches, furs, and precious and semiprecious stones	$1,000 for loss by theft
Firearms of any type	$2,000 for loss by theft
Silver and silver-plated ware, gold and gold-plated ware, and pewterware	$2,500 for loss by theft
Property used at any time, in any manner, for any business purpose	$2,500 on premises $250 off premises
Electronic apparatus, such as a citizens band radio or tape deck that can be plugged into a cigarette lighter, while in or upon a motor vehicle or other motorized land conveyance, if it can be powered by the electronic system of, or another source of power within, the vehicle or conveyance	$1,000 including accessories, antennas, tapes, wires, records, discs, or other medical for use with this electronic apparatus

Automobile Insurance

PAP DECLARATIONS PAGE EXCERPTS
(Covers both automobiles)

Smiths' Coverage							
Coverages, Limits of liability and Premiums. Coverage is provided only where a premium or limit of liability is shown for the coverage.							

Auto	A-Liability in thousands	B-Medical payments each person		C-Uninsured motorists in thousands	D-Damage to you auto Actual cash value minus deductible		Towing and labor per disablement
					[1]Collision loss	[2]Other than collision loss	
	$300	$10,000		$300	$500	$250	$100

Auto	Cov A	Cov B	Cov C	Cov D-1	Cov D-2	Towing	Supp Cov	Auto Total
Premium	$400	$100	$150	$100	$70	$10		$830 per 6 months

Part D Exclusions	
	Public or Livery Use - exclusion of loss while the auto is being used to carry persons or property for a fee unless it is being used as a share-the-expense car pool.
	Wear and Tear - Coverage does not apply to damage due and confined to (1) wear and tear, (2) freezing, (3) mechanical or electrical breakdown or failure, or (4) road damage to tires.
	War and Other Catastrophic Losses - Exclusions include loss resulting from radioactive contamination; the discharge of a nuclear weapon, accidental or not; ware, declared or not; civil war; insurrection; and rebellion or revolution.
	Campers or Trailers - Exclusions include coverage for any trailer or camper body owned by the named insured and not described in the declarations.
	Governmental Action - Coverage does not apply to loss to any covered vehicle that is destroyed or confiscated by governmental or civil authorities.
	Equipment-Related Exclusions - Exclusions apply to the following types of equipment: 1. Electronic equipment designed for the reproduction of sound or the reception and transmission of audio visual or data signals, including media and accessories. 2. Awnings, cabanas, and equipment used to create additional living facilities. 3. Equipment designed or used for locating or detecting radar or laser beams. 4. Customizing equipment and furnishings.
	Nonowned Auto Exclusions - Exclusions apply to the following autos not owned by the named insured. 1. Loss to any nonowned auto when the auto is used by the named insured or family member without having the reasonable belief that he/she is entitled to do so. 2. Loss to any nonowned auto being maintained or used by any person while employed or otherwise engaged in the business of selling, repairing, servicing, storing, or parking vehicles designed for use on public highways, including road testing and delivery. 3. Loss to any nonowned auto being maintained or used by any person while employed or otherwise engaged in a business other than the auto business listed in the above exclusion.
	Racing and Speed Contests - Coverage does not apply to otherwise covered autos if they are damaged while involved in racing or speed contests.
	Rental Vehicles - Physical damage coverage qualifies coverage for damage to rental vehicles otherwise covered as nonowned autos.
	Transportation Expenses - Applies only in the event of total theft of a covered auto.
	Limit of Liability - The amount actually paid by the insurer is limited to (1) actual cash value of the damaged or stolen property or (2) the amount required to repair or replace it - whichever is less.

	Payment of Loss - The insurer reserves the right, in the event of a covered physical damage loss, to pay the loss in money or to repair the property.
	No Benefit to Bailee - The insurance will not benefit, directly or indirectly, any person who assumes control of a covered auto for business purposes.
	Other Sources of Recovery - When other sources of recovery are also available to cover a loss to a covered owned auto or its equipment, it is a condition of the other sources of recovery provision that the insurer pay only its share.
	Appraisal - An appraisal may be demanded by either party in the event that the insurer and the insured agree that there is coverage, but disagree on the amount of physical damage loss.
Part E **Duties After an** **Accident or Loss**	In general, the insured is obligated to notify the insurance company promptly following any loss. Notification should include details concerning the loss and submit proof of loss, if necessary. Cooperation is expected of the insured in the investigation, defense, or settlement of any claim or suit. In addition, an insured must take the necessary steps after physical damage loss to protect the auto from further damage. The insurer will reimburse the insured for any reasonable expenses incurred in doing so. Storage charges, if necessary, for a damaged auto might be such a covered expense. In the event that the covered auto is stolen, the insured is required to notify the police immediately. The insured is expected to cooperate in permitting the insurer to inspect and appraise the damaged property before the loss is settled.
Part F **General** **Provisions**	**Bankruptcy** - The insurer must fulfill its obligations under the policy even if the insured declares bankruptcy or insolvency.
	Fraud - The insurer will not cover any insured who makes fraudulent statements or engages in fraudulent conduct in connection with any accident or loss for which a claim is made.
	Legal Action Against the Insurer - The insurer must fully satisfy all the terms of the policy before he/she can bring legal action against the insurer.
	The Insurer's Right To Recover Payment - If any payment is made by the insurer, the insurer may, to the extent of payment, take over the rights of the person to whom payment was made against the negligent third party.
	Policy Period and Territory - Coverage under the PAP applies only to accidents and losses that occur during the policy period and within the US, its territories or possessions, Puerto Rico, or Canada. Coverage also applies to accidents involving the covered auto while being conveyed between ports within the above territory.
	Termination - An insured may cancel the policy at any time by notifying the insurance company. However, an insurer may cancel only under the following circumstances: 1. The named insured fails to pay the premium due. 2. Any insured's drivers license is suspended or revoked. 3. The named insured lied on the application for insurance.

INVESTMENT INFORMATION

During Sue's marriage to Jerry, an education fund was established for Jerry, Jr. and Christopher. These funds were intended for the children's education. Since Jerry died, Sue has no longer contributed to this fund. At the present time, the fund balance is $22,747. The money has been invested short-term at 6%, and the Smiths have the option of renewing the short-term CDs in April at an interest rate of 4%.

When Sue received the life insurance proceeds of $250,000 from Jerry's death in 1994, she asked a broker to help her manage the money. Her broker, John, has her in a wrap account with a 3% annual fee. John has full discretion over the account and determines which securities to buy and sell and when to buy and sell. John's record regarding Sue's investment portfolio over the last five years is as follows:

	1994	1995	1996	1997	1998
Load Adjusted Total Return	(10.0)	?	(8.5)	12.0	3.0

Sue did not have the information for 1995 and has been unable to obtain it from John.

Sue considers herself to be a conservative to moderate investor and has little experience or education in the area of investments. Tom believes that he is a more moderate investor, since he has more experience with investments than Sue.

INCOME TAX INFORMATION

The Smiths are in the 28% marginal tax bracket for Federal income tax and 6% for state income tax.

RETIREMENT INFORMATION

They both plan to retire when Sue reaches 65. They expect the retirement period to be 30 years. They expect their retirement portfolio to average 10% returns, pre-tax. Social Security benefits for Tom today would be $14,000 at full age retirement of 67. The benefits for Sue at age 67 on her own earnings would be $9,600.

ABC sponsors a profit sharing plan and a 401(k) plan. The 401(k) plan allows them to defer up to 16% of their salary with a 3% employer match when they save 6%; maximum deferral is $10,000. Neither Tom nor Sue has ever participated in the 401(k) plan, but both have fully vested balances in the profit sharing plan as follows:

Vested Balance January 1, 1999	
Tom	$80,000
Sue	$12,000

The ABC Profit Sharing Plan allows the participant to choose between self-directing the retirement assets through the available mutual funds or having the company's fund manager manage the assets. The Smiths, not being confident in their ability to manage assets, have chosen to let the fund manager invest their assets. The 401(k) plan can only be self-directed.

The investments and investment options for the 401(k) plan are listed below.

XYZ Small Company Growth Fund	
Fund Objective:	The Fund seeks long-term growth of capital.
Portfolio Concept:	The Fund invests primarily in common stock of small and medium sized companies that are early in their life cycle and have the potential to become major enterprises.

XYZ Growth Fund	
Fund Objective:	The Fund seeks growth of capital and, secondarily, income.
Portfolio Concept:	The Fund seeks to invest in equity securities placing primary emphasis on those securities, which Fund Management believes to be undervalued. The Fund may invest up to 20% in foreign securities.

XYZ Index Trust	
Fund Objective:	The Fund seeks to approximate the total return of the S&P 500 Composite Stock Price Index.
Portfolio Concept:	The Fund invests primarily in a portfolio of equity securities (stocks) that are included in the S&P 500 Index.

XYZ Foreign Fund	
Fund Objective:	The Fund seeks long-term capital growth through investments in stocks and debt obligations of companies and governments outside the United States.
Portfolio Concept:	The Fund generally invests in common stocks; however, it may also invest in preferred stocks and certain debt securities, rated or unrated, such as convertible bonds and bonds selling at a discount.

XYZ Balanced Fund	
Fund Objective:	The Fund seeks the highest total investment return consistent with prudent risk.
Portfolio Concept:	The Fund has a fully managed investment policy utilizing equity, debt, and convertible securities.

XYZ Income Fund	
Fund Objective:	The Fund seeks a high level of income, consistent with the prudent investment of capital, through a flexible investment program emphasizing high-grade bonds.
Portfolio Concept:	The Fund invests primarily in a broad range of high-grade, income-producing securities such as corporate bonds and government securities

XYZ Money Market Fund	
Fund Objective:	The Fund seeks preservation of capital, current income and liquidity.
Portfolio Concept:	The Fund is a money market mutual fund that seeks capital preservation, current income and liquidity through investment in a portfolio of high-quality, short-term money market instruments, including securities issued by the U.S. government, its agencies, or instrumentalities.

The company has made the following contributions to the profit sharing plan for Tom and Sue for each of the related years:

	Tom	Sue
1999	none yet	none yet
1998	$15,000	$3,600
1997	$ 0	$ 0
1996	$13,605	$3,265
1995	$10,366	$2,488
1994	$ 8,954	$2,369
Balance 1/1/94	$25,000	$ 0

All contributions are made December 31st of the indicated year.

ANNUALIZED RETURNS OF RETIREMENT FUNDS

	1988	1989	1990	1991	1992	1993	1994	1995	1996	1997	1998
XYZ Small Co. Growth Fund	-	-	-	-	-	-	-	-	4.83%	41.17%	15.01%
XYZ Growth Fund	-	-	-	32.96%	0.03%	25.20%	9.97%	32.37%	1.77%	36.82%	14.50%
XYZ Index Trust	-	-	-	-	-	-	-	9.66%	1.02%	37.23%	13.25%
XYZ Foreign Fund	28.77%	24.75%	21.99%	30.53%	-3.01%	18.25%	0.10%	36.82%	0.35%	11.15%	7.08%
XYZ Balanced Fund	19.89%	4.60%	17.04%	22.98%	1.08%	24.69%	5.03%	13.71%	0.91%	32.87%	11.60%
XYZ Income Fund	14.75%	0.74%	8.91%	12.75%	8.32%	17.32%	6.74%	12.58%	-4.43%	18.54%	9.21%
XYZ Money Market Fund	4.21%	3.87%	4.01%	5.02%	5.40%	4.75%	5.00%	5.25%	6.01%	6.71%	5.20%

Note: Blank performance years are before inception of the fund.

GIFTS, ESTATES, TRUSTS, AND WILL INFORMATION

They have not considered any estate planning nor do they have wills.

STATEMENT OF CASH FLOWS

Tom and Sue Smith
Statement of Cash Flows
Projected for 1999

CASH INFLOWS

Salaries

Tom's		$100,000
Sue's		24,000
	Total Salaries	$124,000

Investment Income

ML Brokerage Account		$ 3,050
Sue's Investment Portfolio		4,771
Savings Account		618
Sue's Education Fund		1,062
	Investment Income	$ 9,501

Total Cash Inflows	**$133,501**

CASH OUTFLOWS

Living Expenses

Food		$ 4,300
Clothing		4,000
Entertainment		6,500
Utilities, Cable, and Phone		5,000
Auto Maintenance		1,200
Church		2,000
Home Mortgage		14,934
Auto Loans		18,818
Credit Card		4,300
	Total Living Expenses	$ 61,052

Insurance

Health		$ 2,400
Auto		1,660
Life		520
Homeowners		920
Fur & Jewelry Endorsement		30
Disability		1,677
	Total Insurance	$ 7,207

Taxes

Property (Residence)		$ 4,936
Federal Income (Withholdings)		37,200
State Income		4,000
Payroll (FICA) (Schedule 1)		7,787
	Total Taxes	$ 53,923

Total Cash Outflows	**$122,182**
Discretionary Cash Flow	**$ 11,319**

Schedule 1:

OASDI

Tom	$72,600 x 6.2%	=	$4,501
Sue	$24,000 x 6.2%	=	1,488

HI

Tom	$100,000 x 1.45%	=	1,450
Sue	$24,000 x 1.45%	=	348
Total			**$7,787**

STATEMENT OF FINANCIAL POSITION

Tom and Sue Smith
Balance Sheet
As of January 1, 1999

ASSETS[1]

Liquid Assets

			LIABITILES[2] AND NET WORTH		
			Short-Term Liabilities		
JT	Checking[6]	$ 7,500	W Credit Cards	$ 4,300	
JT	Savings[7]	15,450			
	Total Liquid Assets	$ 22,950	*Long-Term Liabilities*		
	Invested Assets		JT Home Mortgage	$144,981	
H	First Mutual Growth Fund[8]	$ 7,950	H/W Auto Loans	40,069	
H	ML Brokerage Account[3]	100,000	H Margin Loan[5]	7,500	
W	Sue's Investment Port.	210,000	Total L-T	$192,550	
W	Sue's Education Fund	22,747			
H	Tom's Profit Sharing Plan	80,000	**Total Liabilities**	$196,850	
W	Sue's Profit Sharing Plan	12,000			
H	Tom's IRA[4]	9,000			
	Total Invested Assets	$441,697			
	Use Assets				
JT	Home	$185,000	**Net Worth**	$552,797	
H	Lexus	32,000			
W	BMW	21,000			
H	Boat	10,000			
W	Furs and Jewelry	10,000			
JT	Furniture and Household	27,000			
	Total Use Assets	$285,000	**Total Liabilities**		
	Total Assets	$749,647	**and Net Worth**	$749,647	

Notes to Financial Statements:

1 All assets are stated at fair market value.
2 Liabilities are stated at principal only.
3 ML Brokerage Account is stated at gross value, which does not include margin loan of $7,500.
4 Tom's IRA is currently invested in CDs at a local bank.
5 Margin loan is for ML Brokerage Account. Interest rate is currently 8%.
6 The checking account is a non-interest bearing account.
7 The savings account earns 4% per year.
8 See detail of fund.

H = Husband
W = Wife
JT = Joint tenancy

INFORMATION REGARDING ASSETS AND LIABILITIES

Investment Income

ML Brokerage Account	
MM	$ 300
Bonds	3,350
Margin Interest	(600)
	$3,050
Sue's Investment Portfolio	
Bonds	$1,300
Stocks	3,471
	$4,771
Savings Account	$ 618
Sue's Education Fund	$1,062
TOTAL	**$9,501**

House

Principal Residence	January 1, 1996 (Purchase)
FMV (Current)	$185,000
Original Loan	$148,000
Term	30 years
Interest Rate	9.5%
Payment	$1,244.46
Remaining Mortgage	$144,981
Remaining Term	27 years

Boat

The original purchase price of the boat was $10,000. It is completely paid for. The boat is a 90 horsepower fishing boat.

Automobiles

	Tom's 1998 Lexus	Sue's 1997 BMW
Purchase Price	$40,000	$35,000
Down Payment	$0	$10,000
Term	48 months	48 months
Interest Rate	7%	8%
Monthly Payment	$957.85	$610.32
Payments Remaining	33	20
Balance	$28,677.07	$11,392.23

ML Brokerage Account

Account Name: Thomas Smith				
Account Number: AB100402				
BALANCES				
MONEY MARKET	**PRICE/ SHARE**	**SHARES**	**CURRENT YIELD**	**FMV**
Money Market	$1.00	7,324.71	4.5%	$7,324.71
BONDS	**MATURITY**	**COUPON**	**COST BASIS**	**FMV**
10,000 US Treasury Note	5	7.5%	$10,351.18	$10,000.00
15,000 US Treasury Bond	25	6.0%	13,138.64	10,579.83
50,000 US Treasury Bond	30	0.0%	4,093.40	3,982.02
20,000 Davidson Debenture	20	8.5%	17,455.93	16,288.44
			$45,039.15	$40,850.29
STOCKS	**PRICE/ SHARE**	**SHARES**	**COST BASIS**	**FMV**
Stock 1*	$5.20	2,000	$10,000	$10,400
Stock 2*	$4.85	1,500	6,750	7,275
Stock 3*	$26.00	500	11,250	13,000
			$28,000	$30,675
* These stocks do not currently pay dividends.				
MUTUAL FUNDS	**PRICE/ SHARE**	**SHARES**	**COST BASIS**	**FMV**
Emerging Growth Fund	$21.00	500	$12,250	$10,500
Balanced Fund	$18.00	425	8,925	7,650
Municipal Bond Fund	$12.00	250	3,500	3,000
			$24,675	$21,150
Note: All distributions from these funds are reinvested.				
OPTIONS	**# OF OPTIONS CONTRACTS**	**OPTION PREMIUM**	**EXERCISE PRICE**	**OPTION EXPIRATION**
Stock 2 Call Options	5	$3.00	$5.50	July 99
Stock 3 Put Options	5	$5.00	$24.00	March 99
MARGIN BALANCE				
OUTSTANDING BALANCE				$7,500
NET ACCOUNT VALUE				**$92,500**
TOTAL ACCOUNT VALUE				**$100,000**

First Mutual Growth Fund

Account Name: Thomas Smith Account Number: AB100357						
Transaction	Date	Amount	Price/ Share	Shares	Total Shares	Total Value
Buy	04/01/97	$ 2,500	$25.00	100	100	$ 2,500
Buy	08/01/97	$ 4,000	$20.00	200	300	$ 6,000
Reinvest Div	12/01/97	$ 500	$12.50	40	340	$ 4,250
Buy	02/01/98	$ 3,000	$15.00	200	540	$ 8,100
Buy	04/01/98	$ 2,000	$20.00	100	640	$12,800
Buy	06/01/98	$ 1,500	$25.00	60	700	$17,500
Sell	12/01/98	$11,880	$27.00	(440)	260	$ 7,020
Reinvest Div	12/01/98	$ 1,080	$27.00	40	300	$ 8,100
BALANCE	12/31/98	--	$26.50	--	300	$ 7,950

Note: All income from this fund is reinvested.

Sue's Investment Portfolio

Bonds

Bonds	Term	Duration	Current FMV
10,000 U.S. Treasury Bonds	10	7.12 years	$10,000
5,000 U.S. Treasury Bonds	20	9.95 years	$ 5,000
		Total Value of Bonds	$15,000

Stocks

Shares	Stock	$\bar{x}$	Beta	σ	R^2	P/E Ratio	Dividend Yield	Basis	FMV
1,000	Stock A	6%	0.65	11%	75	13.0	3.0%	$30,000	$38,000
575	Stock B	11%	0.75	9%	65	14.0	3.7%	$45,000	$46,000
200	Stock C	7%	0.65	10%	30	15.1	3.7%	$20,000	$17,000
500	Stock D	3%	0.70	8%	45	25.2	0.0%	$11,000	$8,500
1,000	Stock E	25%	0.95	15%	70	14.4	0.0%	$20,000	$18,000
1,250	Stock F	22%	1.10	18%	20	11.1	0.0%	$23,000	$25,000
							Total Value of Stocks		$152,500

Mutual Funds

Shares	Mutual Fund	Style	$\bar{x}$	Alpha	Beta	σ	R^2	Front End Load	Expense Ratio	Basis	FMV
210	Fund A	MG	14%	3%	1.1	12%	57	8.5%	.71%	$ 2,500	$ 2,625
300	Fund B	LG	11.5%	.5%	0.94	8%	81	8.5%	1.0%	$ 5,000	$ 5,100
443	Fund C	MV	6%	(4%)	0.65	8%	42	8.5%	3.5%	$10,000	$11,075
1,000	Fund D	MG	-6%	(10%)	0.70	20%	4	8%	7.0%	$ 8,000	$ 7,500
320	Fund E	LG	4%	(3%)	1.1	5%	60	5%	2.5%	$ 9,500	$ 8,000
410	Fund F	LG	7%	(2.5%)	0.9	3%	78	3%	1.5%	$10,000	$ 8,200
								Total Value of Mutual Funds			$42,500

Note: All income distributions from the mutual funds is reinvested.

TOTAL PORTFOLIO VALUE	**$210,000**

Key	
$\bar{x}$	5 Year Average Return
σ	Standard Deviation
R^2	Coefficient of Determination
L	Large
M	Medium
G	Growth
V	Value

QUESTIONS

1.   List the Smiths' financial strengths and weaknesses.

    a.   Strengths:

    b.   Weaknesses:

2.   After reading the case, what additional information would you request from the Smiths to complete your data-gathering phase?

3.   Calculate the following financial ratios for the Smiths.

$$\frac{\text{Liquid Assets}}{\text{Monthly Expenses}} \quad =$$

$$\frac{\text{Liquid Assets}}{\text{Current Monthly Debt Payments}} \quad =$$

$$\frac{\text{Net Worth}}{\text{Total Assets}} \quad =$$

$$\frac{\text{Total Debt}}{\text{Total Assets}} \quad =$$

$$\frac{\text{Total Debt}}{\text{Annual Total Income}} \quad =$$

$$\frac{\text{Housing}}{\text{Monthly Gross Income}} \quad =$$

$$\frac{\text{Housing \& Monthly Debt Payments}}{\text{Monthly Gross Income}} \quad =$$

$$\frac{\text{Investment Assets}}{\text{Annual Gross Income}} \quad =$$

$$\frac{\text{Monthly Savings}}{\text{Monthly Gross Income}} \quad =$$

4.   Comment on any of the above ratios that you think are important.

5.   What is the taxable gain on the sale of the 440 shares of First Mutual
        Growth Fund (December 1, 1998) and how will it be classified for income
        tax purposes?   Assume that the taxable basis in the shares sold is
        determined using a FIFO method.

6.   What are other methods of determining the taxable basis of the 440
        shares of First Mutual Growth Fund sold on December 1, 1998?

7.   As of January 1, 1999, what is the average basis per share for the shares remaining of First Mutual Growth Fund, assuming the FIFO method was used for determining the sale of the 440 shares?

8.   As of December 1, 1998, what is the internal rate of return for the First Mutual Growth Fund since the Smiths first purchase on April 1, 1997?

9.   Discuss the coverage of personal property including the boat.

10.   Under the loss of use coverage, for an HO2 policy, what is usually provided?

11.   How does a change in the price of the below listed stocks impact the value of the related option? Each change (A-D) is independent.

ML Brokerage Account			
	Stock	*Price Changes To*	*Option Profit*
Change A	Stock 2	$6.00	
Change B	Stock 2	$4.00	
Change C	Stock 3	$29.00	
Change D	Stock 3	$20.00	

12.   Assume the Smiths want to treat their children equally in the event of their deaths, but do not know how to provide for any possible unborn children. Discuss the most appropriate technique to accomplish this objective.

13.   Calculate the geometric average return for each of the funds in the ABC retirement plan.

14.   Determine the Sharpe and Treynor performance measures for each fund in Sue's investment portfolio. Assume a risk free rate equal to the one-year T-bill rate.

15.   Rank each of the funds in Sue's investment portfolio by the Sharpe and Treynor index.   Comment on why the order might be the same or different for the two measures and what the index numbers mean.

16.   What is the coupon rate for each of the two bonds in Sue's portfolio?

17.   Comment on the allocation of mutual funds among the different management approaches and asset sizes.

18.   Comment on Sue's broker's choice of mutual funds in her portfolio.

19.   How well have Tom and Sue's investments in the profit sharing plan at ABC Company performed since January 1, 1994?

20.   Comment on the Smiths' decision to let ABC's money manager have control over their retirement assets. What should they do now?

21.   If the Smiths had earned an average return equal to that of the XYZ
       Balanced Fund you just calculated, how much better off would they be?

22.   What should be the value of the following bonds in the ML Brokerage
       Account if all interest rates decrease by 1%? Assume interest is paid
       semi-annually.

       a.   10,000 U.S. Treasury Note

       b.   15,000 U.S. Treasury Bond

       c.   50,000 U.S. Treasury Bond

23.   Is the current yield curve consistent with the liquidity premium theory?
       Why or why not?

24.   Is the current yield curve consistent with the market segmentation theory? Why or why not?

25.   What was the rate of return on Sue's investment portfolio in 1995?

26.   If the interest rates for all maturities increase by 1.0%, what will be the approximate value of the bonds in Sue's investment portfolio?

27.   Determine the duration of each of the bonds in the ML Brokerage Account.

28.   What is the percentage and dollar investment gain that Tom would receive if the price of Stock 2 increases to $7.50 (in Brokerage Account)?

29.   Has Tom done an effective job of immunizing Stock 3 from downside risk? Why or why not?

30.   Sue has decided that the CDs and her investment account will be used for funding the cost of college for the boys. Sue wants to set aside enough of these assets to fund their education with the remainder being used to fund Kelsey's college education. Ignoring the transaction costs of selling the current assets, how much does she need to set aside for the boys' college if she wants to invest in an even mix of 5- and 10-year Treasury bonds? Assume all taxes will be paid out of current expenditures.

31.   Sue wants to know if she and Tom need to contribute to a fund for Kelsey's education and how much they need to contribute over the next 15 years. Their first contribution will be in one year and they will invest in a portfolio that is split equally between the S&P 500 and 5-year Treasury bonds. This allocation will be maintained by rebalancing every six months. Assume the tax on earnings will be paid from their salary and not from the education fund.

32.   If Tom were to become disabled on May 30, 1999, when would he collect benefits and how much would he receive in benefits during 1999?

33.   What are the tax consequences to the receipt of disability benefits?

34.   How much of the Smiths' current net worth is available to be invested for their retirement goals?

35.   How much of their current gross income in dollars and percentages are the Smiths currently saving toward their retirement goal?

36.   What are the Smiths' expected Social Security benefits for Tom at age 62 and Sue at age 65?

37.   Does it appear that they will be better off with Sue collecting Social Security retirement benefits from Tom's earnings or from her own?

38.   To meet their expected goal at retirement, how much money should the Smiths have accumulated assuming a capital needs analysis using the annuity approach?

39.   To meet their expected goal at retirement, how much money should the Smiths have accumulated assuming a capital needs analysis using the capital preservation approach?

40.   To meet their expected goal at retirement, how much money should the Smiths have accumulated assuming a capital needs analysis using the purchasing power preservation approach?

41.   What do the Smiths need to do now to meet their retirement income goal?

42.   Will the Smiths benefit from itemizing deductions on their 1998 income tax return? If so, what type of interest deductions can they take?

43.   Determine the Smiths' 1998 tax liability. Assume the same income, etc. from the 1999 cash flow statement. Are they over or under withheld?

44.   Discuss the Smiths' current life insurance situation.

45.   Calculate Tom's gross estate were he to die today.

46.   What are the current estate planning deficiencies?

47.   Do they qualify for refinancing their home mortgage?

48.   Calculate the payments and savings from the alternative ways to refinance.

49.   What would their payments have to be if they just kept the same loan and paid it over the remaining 15 years? The Smiths' desire to be debt free in 15 years (see goal #6).

JOSEPH AND CINDY SLEIGH

CASE SCENARIO AND QUESTIONS

JOSEPH AND CINDY SLEIGH

Table of Contents

JOSEPH AND CINDY SLEIGH

Case Scenario and Questions

Joseph and Cindy have come to you, a financial planner, for help in developing a plan to accomplish their financial goals. From your initial meeting together, you have gathered the following information. Assume today is January 1, 1999.

PERSONAL INFORMATION

Joseph Sleigh *(Age 65)*

Joseph is in excellent health. He owns Sleigh's Big-N-Tall, Inc., a men's store focusing on men's attire for larger clients. Joseph's salary is $250,000. Sleigh's employs 25 full-time and 10 part-time employees.

Cindy Sleigh (Age 50)

Cindy is in excellent health. She is a CPA and is employed by an international accounting firm, where she is currently a manager in the area of healthcare consulting. She has a daughter, Beverly, from a former marriage who is 30 and living on her own. Cindy's salary is $50,000.

The Sleighs

They have been married for 25 years.

Children

Joseph and Cindy have three children from their marriage in addition to Beverly.

Susie	Age 23
David	Age 21
Mary	Age 5
Beverly	Age 30 is Cindy's child from a previous marriage

Helga Smatters

Cindy's mother, Helga, turned 71 on December 1, 1998, and is a widower with a substantial net worth. In addition to sizable holdings of real estate, stocks, and bonds, Helga has $450,000 in her IRA rollover account as of December 31, 1998 (her account grew by $25,000 during 1998). Because she is in extremely poor health, she had an attorney draft a will leaving her entire estate to Cindy. The will provides that if Cindy should disclaim any or all of the inheritance, the disclaimed portion will be left in trust for Cindy's four children.

PERSONAL AND FINANCIAL OBJECTIVES

1. Joseph plans to sell his business and retire immediately. He expects to live 30 years.
2. Joseph wants to continue to transfer some of his wealth to his children to avoid estate taxes. He will consider using the family limited partnership that is currently in place.

ECONOMIC INFORMATION

General

The Sleighs expect inflation to average 4.0% annually both currently and for the long-term.

U.S. Treasury
Current Yield Curve

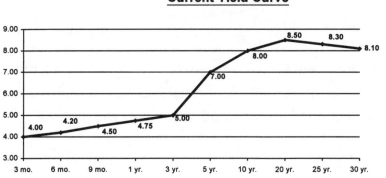

Economic Outlook-Investments

	Expected Returns (pre-tax)		Expected Standard Deviation
Aggressive stocks	18%	±	15%
Growth stocks	14%	±	10%
S & P 500	11%	±	8%
Bonds	8%	±	3%
Insurance Contracts	6%	±	2%
Money markets	5%	±	1%
T-Bill	4%	±	1%

Banking

The Sleighs have favorable banking relationships and are able to borrow money for any purpose at the following rates:

Type of Loan	Rates
Installment loans-secured	6.5%
Personal signature bank loans	9.0%
Mortgage Loan - 30 year fixed	8.5%
Mortgage Loan - 15 year fixed	8.0%

INVESTMENT INFORMATION

The Sleighs consider $100,000 adequate for an emergency fund. They indicate a moderate level of risk tolerance in investments.

INCOME TAX INFORMATION

The Sleighs are in a marginal tax bracket of 39.6% for Federal and 6% for state. They pay on average 31% and 5% for Federal and state tax, respectively. Capital gains are taxed at 20% for Federal (no difference for state tax).

INSURANCE INFORMATION

Life Insurance	Policy 1	Policy 2
Insured	Joseph Sleigh	Joseph Sleigh
Face amount	$1,500,000	$250,000
Cash value	$25,000	$15,000
Type of policy	Whole Life	Whole Life
Annual premium	$4,500	$3,500
Beneficiary	Beverly, Susie, David, Mary	Cindy Sleigh
Contingent beneficiary	Joseph's Estate	Sleigh Children's Trust
Policy owner	Sleigh Children's Trust*	Cindy Sleigh
Settlement options	N/A	Single Life Annuity (guaranteed for 10 years)

*The original owner of policy 1 was Joseph. It was transferred to the trust on June 30, 1998. William Bradley, who has been a friend of Joseph since college, is the trustee for the Children's Trust. The cash value at the date of transfer was $25,000. The policy was purchased January 1, 1990.

Cindy also has term insurance provided through her employer. She has selected $100,000 of coverage. The primary beneficiary on her term insurance is Joseph.

Health Insurance
Joseph: Currently has a good health insurance plan through Sleigh's Big-N-Tall, but will not be covered once any sale of the business has been finalized. Joseph's health plan has the following features: • $1,000 individual deductible   • $2,500 family deductible   • $3,500 stop loss provision   • 80% coinsurance clause   • $5 million major medical limit
Cindy: Coverage is available through her employer, but she is covered under Joseph's policy.

Disability Insurance

Joseph does not have disability insurance coverage.

Cindy has disability coverage provided through her employer, 60% coverage, own occupation, 180-day elimination period.

Property and Liability Auto (both cars) Insurance

Type	PAP
Liability (Bodily injury)	$100,000/$300,000
Property Damage	$50,000
Medical Payments	$1,000
Physical Damage, own car	Actual Cash Value
Uninsured Motorist	$100,000/$300,000
Collision Deductible	$1,000
Comprehensive Deductible	$500
Annual Premium (2 cars)	$1,800

Homeowners Insurance

Type	HO3
Dwelling	$700,000
Other structures	$70,000
Personal Property	$350,000
Personal Liability	$100,000
Medical Payments	$1,000
Deductible	$100
Co Insurance Clause	80/20
Annual Premium	$2,200

Umbrella Liability Insurance

The policy has a face value of $3 million with a premium of $500 per year.

RETIREMENT INFORMATION

Joseph

- Joseph has a profit sharing plan and a money purchase pension plan at Sleigh's Big-N-Tall, Inc., with a combined balance of $1,350,000.
- Joseph also has an IRA account with a balance of $30,000 (see details). The IRA plan was established in 1984.
- Cindy is the beneficiary of all of Joseph's retirement accounts.

Cindy

- Cindy has a 401(k) plan in which she is able to defer up to 20% of her salary. The accounting firm matches $0.25 for each $1.00 she defers, up to 6% of her salary (firm's total match is 1.5% of compensation). Joseph is the beneficiary of all of Cindy's retirement accounts.
- Joseph and Cindy are retiring today and both expect to live until age 95.
- Joseph and Cindy have estimated that they need $250,000 per year, in today's dollars, for retirement. This amount would drop by 25% if only one was alive.

Asset Allocation

The Sleighs plan to create a separate portfolio to provide for their retirement income. They expect to maintain a retirement portfolio with the following asset allocation.

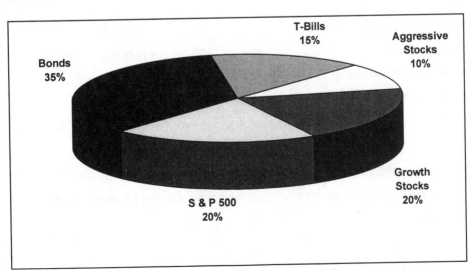

EDUCATION INFORMATION

Susie and David are both enrolled in Harvard University. The tuition is currently $30,000 for each child and is expected to increase by approximately 7% per year. This cost is being funded by Joseph and Cindy from current earnings and savings. They are concerned about funding Mary's education, because Joseph and Cindy are retiring and will not be working while Mary is in school. Mary is extremely gifted and will likely attend an Ivy League school. They expect tuition to be $30,000 (today's cost) and to increase by 7% each year. They expect Mary, beginning at age 18, will attend four years of undergraduate and two years of graduate school. They would like to set aside the money today, which would be invested in bonds, to fund the cost of Mary's college education.

INFORMATION REGARDING WILLS, TRUSTS, AND ESTATES

Wills

Both Joseph and Cindy have wills. Each of the wills provides for all of the assets to be left in a QTIP trust with the surviving spouse as the income beneficiary and the children as the remaindermen. The Sleighs believe they need to have their wills updated.

The Sleigh Family Trust

The Sleigh Family Trust was established in 1986 for the purpose of reducing the Sleighs' estate tax. The primary beneficiaries of the trust are the four children with the contingent beneficiary being the American Cancer Society. If a child should die, that proportional interest would pass to that child's heirs. If no heir exists, then the interest would pass equally to the remaining children of the trust. If all children should die without heirs, then the American Cancer Society would immediately receive the entire corpus of the trust. The trust is currently valued at $3,000,000.

Gifts

Joseph has made the following taxable gifts to the Sleigh Family Trust for the benefit of his children.

Date	Taxable Gift	Gift tax paid*	Date Paid	
07/31/86	$ 400,000	$ 0		
04/02/92	500,000	114,000	April 15, 1993	
11/07/94	350,000	141,500	April 15, 1995	
10/04/95	150,000	64,500	April 15, 1996	
08/23/96	75,000	32,250	April 15, 1997	
05/06/97	100,000	44,500	April 15, 1998	
06/05/98	200,000	80,750	April 15, 1999	Due
	$1,775,000	$477,500		

*All gift taxes were paid April 15th of the year following the year of the gift.

The Sleigh Children's Insurance Trust (All 4 children)

This trust was set up in early 1998 for the purpose of reducing the Sleigh's estate tax liability. On June 30, 1998, Joseph Sleigh transferred life insurance Policy 1 to the trust. There is a Crummey provision provided for in the trust document.

JOCI Family Limited Partnership (JO = Joseph; CI = Cindy; JOCI = JO + CI)

Sid Johnson, one of the area's best estate planning attorneys, discussed the benefits of setting up a Family Limited Partnership with the Sleighs. With his help, the Sleighs established JOCI Family Limited Partnership (JOCI FLP) in 1996. All of the assets transferred to the trust consisted of Joseph's separate property. Joseph currently owns 100% of the JOCI FLP but intends to begin transferring some of the ownership to his children and possibly to Cindy.

STATEMENT OF FINANCIAL POSITION

Joseph and Cindy Sleigh
Statement of Financial Position
As of December 31, 1998

ASSETS[1]				LIABILITIES AND NET WORTH	
Cash/Cash Equivalents				**Liabilities[2]**	
H	Cash and Checking[7]	$ 250,000	W	Credit card balances[3]	$ 15,000
H	Money Market Fund[8]	875,000	H	Short-term note	230,000
	Total Cash/Equivalents	$1,125,000		Auto note balances	0
				Mortgage note	0
				Total Liabilities	$ 245,000
Invested Assets					
H	Profit Sharing-Keogh	$1,350,000			
H	IRA-Joseph	30,000			
W	Cindy - 401(k)	150,000			
H	Growth Mutual Fund	53,100			
H	Due from JOCI	70,500			
H	JOCI Family Limited Partnership (capital)	1,193,600			
H	Common Stock Portfolio[5]	100,000			
H	Sleigh's Big-N-Tall, Inc. Common Stock[6]	2,250,000			
	Total Invested Assets	$5,197,200		Net Worth	$7,519,200
Use Assets					
JT	Residence[4]	$1,000,000			
JT	Personal Property	400,000			
JT	Autos	42,000			
	Total Use Assets	$1,442,000			
Total Assets		$7,764,200		**Total Liabilities & Net Worth**	$7,764,200

Notes:

1 Presented at fair market value.

2 All liabilities are stated at principal only. All non-identified liabilities are jointly owned.

3 Credit card interest rate is 18%.

4 Adjusted taxable basis of home $200,000 (Joseph contributed 75% and Cindy contributed 25% to the purchase of the house).

5 Publicly traded stock.

6 The value is an approximation of the value of the business made by Mr. Sleigh. The company is a C-Corporation with an adjusted taxable basis of $25,000.

7 Cash and checking earn 3% annually.

8 The money market fund earns 5% annually.

Ownership-Title: H = Husband only; W = Wife only; JT = Joint tenants with survivorship rights

STATEMENT OF CASH FLOWS

Joseph and Cindy Sleigh
1998 Statement of Cash Flow
January 1, 1998 to December 31, 1998

INFLOWS - ANNUAL

Joseph's Salary	$250,000	
Cindy's Salary	50,000	
Dividend Income	5,350	
Interest Income	51,250	
Total Inflows		$356,600

OUTFLOWS - ANNUAL

Savings and Investments	$ 56,600	$ 56,600
Fixed Outflows - Annual		
Mortgage (P&I)	$ 0	
Property Taxes	20,000	
Homeowners Insurance	2,200	
Utilities	7,800	
Telephone	600	
Auto (P&I) Pmt	0	
Auto Insurance	1,800	
Life Insurance Policy 2*	3,500	
Gas/Oil/Maintenance	1,800	
Credit Card Payments	8,500	
Umbrella Insurance	500	$ 46,700
Variable Outflows		
Taxes[1]	$119,691	
Food	7,800	
Medical/Dental	2,000	
Clothing/Personal Care	6,000	
Child Care	5,200	
Entertainment/Vacation	10,000	
College	60,000	
Kindergarten	6,000	$216,691
Total Outflows		$319,991
Discretionary Cash Flow		$ 36,609

[1]Notes on taxes

FICA - Joseph	$ 7,866
FICA - Cindy	3,825
Fed - Joseph	77,500
Fed W/H - Cindy	15,500
State - Joseph	12,500
State - Cindy	2,500
	$119,691

*Transfers to trust for life insurance policy one are from discretionary cash flows.

INFORMATION REGARDING ASSETS AND LIABILITIES

Sleigh's Big-N-Tall, Inc.	
	Cash Flow (NOI)
Year 1	$400,000
Year 2	$420,000
Year 3	$435,000
Year 4	$440,000
Terminal Value	$3,000,000*

*The terminal value is calculated by dividing the forecasted NOI for Year 5 of $450,000 by an assumed discount rate of 15%.

Detailed Investment Portfolio (These are not in the Family Limited Partnership)

Balanced Mutual Fund				
Account Name: IRA for Joseph Sleigh			**Account No.:** IRA4340	
Date	**Amount**	**Price/Share**	**Shares**	**Cumulative Balance**
1/1/89 T	$16,000	$40.00	400	400
1/1/90 P	2,000	50.00	40	440
1/1/91 P	2,000	50.00	40	480
T = Transfer P = Purchase				
Account Value as of 12/31/98:			**$30,000**	

Note: The transfer in of $16,000 was the balance from an old 401(k) plan.

Growth Mutual Fund				
Account Name: Joseph Sleigh			**Account No.:** SLE123456	
Date	**Amount**	**Price/Share**	**Shares**	**Balance**
2/1/97				-0-
3/1/97	$7,500	$15.00	500	500
4/1/97	7,500	18.75	400	900
5/1/97	1,000	20.00	50	950
6/1/97	1,000	20.00	50	1,000
7/1/97	1,000	25.00	40	1,040
8/1/97	1,000	25.00	40	1,080
9/1/97	1,000	25.00	40	1,120
10/1/97	1,000	20.00	50	1,170
11/1/97	1,000	25.00	40	1,210
12/1/97	1,000	25.00	40	1,250
3/1/98	2,300	23.00	100	1,350
6/1/98	4,800	24.00	200	1,550
9/1/98	3,000	30.00	100	1,650
12/1/98	6,900*	27.60	250	1,900

*$2,700 was from a reinvested dividend.

Account Value as of 12/31/98:   **$53,100**

Notes:
1 The NAV of the fund on 12/31/97 was $26.00.
2 No dividends were paid in 1997.
3 Dividend of $1.50 per share was paid 12/1/98.
4 The NAV of the fund on December 31, 1998 was $27.9474.

Common Stock Portfolio						
Account Name: Joseph Sleigh						
Stock	**Avg./Exp. Return**	**Price/ Share**	**Total Shares**	**Cost Basis**	**FMV**	**Current Dividend**
A	25%	25.55	1,250.00	7,500	31,937.50	3%
B	23%	37.50	850.00	10,000	31,875.00	4%
C	15%	87.00	175.00	18,000	15,225.00	0%
D	20%	43.00	487.50	16,000	20,962.50	2.5%
Total				51,500	100,000.00	

1 The standard deviation of the portfolio has been 10.9% in the past and is expected to be the same in the future.
2 The stocks which were purchased are as follows:

Stock A	3/5/83
Stock B	4/7/88
Stock C	6/30/98
Stock D	6/30/98

JOCI Family Limited Partnership Investments				
Investment	FMV	Average Expected Return	Standard Deviation	Beta
Growth & Income	$178,000	10.0%	9%	0.92
Balanced	246,500	8.5%	7%	0.72
Foreign	138,500	9.7%	15%	0.30
Brokerage Acct. A	216,000	11.2%	13%	1.22
Brokerage Acct. B	350,000	10.4%	10%	1.12
Total Investments	$1,129,000			

STATEMENT OF FINANCIAL POSITION (JOCI)

JOCI Family Limited Partnership
Statement of Financial Position as of Jan. 1, 1999

ASSETS[1]

Cash/Cash equivalent		
Cash	$45,000	
Money Market	55,000	
Total Cash/Cash Equivalent		$ 100,000
Invested Assets		
Growth and Income Mutual Fund	$178,000	
Balanced Mutual Fund	246,500	
Foreign Mutual Fund	138,500	
Brokerage Account A	216,000	
Brokerage Account B	350,000	
Total Invested Assets		$1,129,000
Use Assets		
Computer Equipment	$4,000	
Luxury Auto	37,500	
Depreciation	(6,400)	
Total Use Assets		$ 35,100
Total Assets		$1,264,100
LIABILITIES		
Due to Joseph Sleigh	$70,500	
Total Liabilities		$ 70,500
Partner's Capital		$1,193,600
Total Liabilities & Partner's Capital		$1,264,100

Notes:

[1] All assets, other than use assets, are stated at fair market value.
[2] Use assets are listed at historical cost.
[3] Depreciation (computer = $4,000 and automobile = $2,400)

QUESTIONS

1.   List the Sleighs' financial strengths and weaknesses.

   a.   Strengths:

   b.   Weaknesses:

2.   After reading the case, what additional information would you request from the Sleighs to complete your data-gathering phase?

3.   Sleigh's Big-N-Tall has been profitable for the past several years. Last year net income was $400,000. If you used a discount rate of 3% above the expected return for aggressive stocks, what would be the value of the business under the capitalized earnings approach?

4.   Because of her financial stability and sizable net worth, Helga Smatters intends to leave the funds in her IRA untouched. When she dies, she believes that these assets will get a step up in basis for her heirs. Comment on her strategy and her beliefs.

5.   Calculate the 1998 and 1999 minimum distributions that are required under IRC Section 401(a)(9) for Helga Smatters. Assume her life expectancy for ages 71 and 72 are 15.3 years and 14.6 years, respectively. Calculate for both the recalculation and non-recalculation methods and assume both distributions will be made in 1999. Assume that her first distribution will be made April 1, 1999.

6.   For the Growth Mutual Fund (listed in the Statement of Financial Position), what is the time weighted return from March 1, 1997 to December 31, 1997?

7.   For the Growth Mutual Fund (listed in the Statement of Financial Position), what is the dollar weighted return from March 1, 1997 to December 31, 1997?

8.   Explain the difference between time-weighted returns and dollar weighted returns.

9. What is Joseph's annualized dollar weighted return for the Growth Mutual Fund (listed in the Statement of Financial Position) as of December 31, 1998?

10. If Joseph sold the shares of the Growth Mutual Fund on January 1, 1999, what would be his after-tax annualized rate of return since he first purchased the shares?

11. If Joseph needs additional cash, what would be the net proceeds from the sale of the Balanced Mutual Fund IRA (listed on his personal Statement of Financial Position), including any taxes and penalties (assume no basis)?

12. What was the gift tax valuation of the life insurance policy transferred to the Sleigh Children's Trust?

13. What is the implication of Joseph's estate being the contingent beneficiary of the life insurance policy #1?

14. What should Joseph have done either prior to, or simultaneously, with the transfer of the life insurance policy #1 to the Sleigh Children's Trust?

15.   What is the implication of Joseph directly paying to the insurer the future premiums for policy #1?

16.   What are the consequences, if instead of directly paying the premiums, Joseph simply adds $4,500 each January 1st to the trust to pay the premiums?

17.   What if Cindy assigns her coverage of the term insurance policy of $100,000 to the Sleigh Children's Trust?

18.   Without regard to any other assets, what has been the benefit of establishing the Sleigh Family Trust?

19.   How much should the Sleighs set aside today for Mary's education?

20.   Assuming both Joseph and Cindy plan to live to age 95, how much money do the Sleighs need today to fund their retirement? Assume a pre-tax portfolio. They will pay income taxes out of the retirement income (assume retirement income pre-tax).

21.   Do the Sleighs have sufficient umbrella liability coverage?

22.   If Joseph were to die today, what assets would be included in his probate estate? Assume the Statement of Financial Position valuations.

23.   Assuming Joseph died today, calculate his gross estate. For purposes of this question, assume funeral and administrative costs total $100,000.

24.   Assuming Joseph died today, calculate his estate tax liability. For purposes of this question, assume funeral and administrative costs total $100,000.

25.   Assuming Cindy died today, what assets would be included in her probate estate?

26.   Assuming Cindy died today, calculate her gross estate. For purposes of this question, assume funeral and administrative costs total $100,000.

27.   Assuming Cindy died today, calculate her estate tax liability.   For purposes of this question, assume funeral and administrative costs total $100,000.

28.   Assume that Joseph dies today and Cindy dies three months later. What is the total estate tax liability of both? Assume funeral and administrative costs are $100,000 each.

29.   Discuss the merits of Joseph creating a CRAT or CRUT and donating his ownership of Big-N-Tall to such a trust as opposed to a direct sale of the business.

30.   Assuming that Joseph has an objective to leave his estate to his heirs but would like to make use of the CRAT or CRUT for retirement income and the charitable tax deduction, what device could he use to replace the assets given to the CRAT or CRUT which would replace the lost assets to his heirs?

31.   If Helga died and Cindy decided to disclaim part or all of any inheritance, what steps should Cindy take to make sure that any such disclaimer was effective?

32.   Referring to the above question, assuming that a disclaimer was not effective (for one reason or another), what would be the consequences to Cindy?

33.   Joseph is contemplating transferring some of his wealth by making an outright gift of an interest in the JOCI Family Limited Partnership as follows:

Cindy	9%
Susie	9%
David	9%
Mary	9%
Beverly	9%
	45%

Determine the amount of additional Federal gift tax Joseph will have to pay if he completes such a transaction today. Assume a minority discount of 35% and that the FMV of JOCI is $1,193,600.

34.   What is the weighted average rate of return of the common stock portfolio?

35.   What is the probability that Joseph's common stock portfolio (listed in the Statement of Financial Position) will have a return above 10.88%?

36.   Joseph decides to purchase a new automobile in the JOCI Family Limited Partnership. The cars in JOCI are used 100% for business. The car he decides to buy costs $85,000. Joseph trades in his old car (listed in the JOCI Statement of Financial Position) and pays cash of $55,000 from the money market account.

     a.   How much gain or loss does JOCI realize?

     b.   How much gain is ultimately reported on Joseph's Form 1040?

     c.   What is the adjusted taxable basis to the partnership of the new car?

37.   If Joseph dies, would his gross estate include the Policy 1 life insurance proceeds?

THIS PAGE IS INTENTIONALLY LEFT BLANK.

BOB AND SHEILA GILLIS

CASE SCENARIO AND QUESTIONS

BOB AND SHEILA GILLIS

Table of Contents

BOB AND SHEILA GILLIS

Case Scenario and Questions

Today is January 1, 1999. Bob and Sheila Gillis have come to you, a financial planner, for help in developing a plan to accomplish their financial goals. From your initial meeting together, you have gathered the following information:

PERSONAL BACKGROUND AND INFORMATION

Bob Gillis (Age 45)

Bob owns an 80% interest in a closely held company, Crescent City Publications. He has recently been diagnosed with cancer and is considering selling the business or transferring some or all of the business to his son Damien.

Sheila Gillis (Age 24)

Sheila is a nurse who works for an orthopedist in the building where Bob has his office.

The Gillises

Bob and Sheila met when Bob sought treatment at the orthopedic clinic after he hurt his back carrying books up to the second floor of his office because there was no elevator. Bob and Sheila have been married for two years. They live in a community property state but have a prenuptial agreement declaring that all property owned is separate property.

The Children

Bob and Sheila have no children together. Bob has two children from a former marriage (spouse is deceased). The children are Angel (Age 18) who is a college student and Damien (Age 27) who works in the publications business with Bob.

PERSONAL AND FINANCIAL OBJECTIVES

1. They plan to retire when Bob reaches age 65.
2. They need adequate retirement income.
3. They want to avoid or minimize death taxes at the death of the first spouse.
4. They want to minimize death taxes at the death of the second spouse.
5. They want to provide adequate estate liquidity.

ECONOMIC INFORMATION

- They expect inflation to average 4.0% annually, both currently and for the long-term.
- They each expect salaries and net income to increase at 4.0% annually, both currently and long-term.
- They believe the S&P 500 is a good measure of the market's performance. It has a historical rate of return of 12%, which is expected to continue.

**Assumed
Treasury Yield Curve**

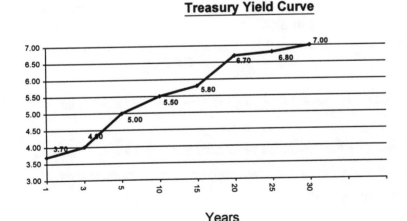

Years

Economic Outlook - Investments

	Return	Standard Deviation
Small Company Stocks	13%	15%
Large Company Stocks	11%	12%
S&P 500	12%	12%
Corporate Bonds	8.5%	6%
Long-term Treasury Bonds	7.0%	5%
T-bills	3.7%	2%

INSURANCE INFORMATION

Life Insurance

	Policy 1	Policy 2	Policy 3[1]
Insured	Bob Gillis	Bob Gillis	Sheila Gillis
Face Amount	$500,000	$150,000	$28,000
Type	Whole life	Term	Term
Cash Value	$5,000	$0	$0
Annual Premium	$1,500	$150	$28
Beneficiary	Sheila Gillis	Sheila Gillis	Bob Gillis
Owner	Bob Gillis	Bob Gillis	Sheila Gillis
Contingent Beneficiary	Estate of Bob Gillis[2]	Estate of Bob Gillis[2]	Damien & Angel

[1] Sheila's term policy is employer provided. The 1999 premium has not been paid.

[2] Bob listed his estate as the contingent beneficiary because he was concerned about his wife's ability to pay off their debt obligations in the event that he should have an untimely death.

Health Insurance

Sheila currently has a health plan provided through her employer. Sheila and Bob are both currently covered by her plan. Sheila's plan has the following characteristics:

- $1,000 individual deductible
- $2,500 family deductible
- $4,000 stop-loss provision
- 80% co-insurance clause
- $3 million major medical limit

Note: Angel is also covered under this plan and is eligible to remain covered until age 25.

Crescent City Publications does not have a health insurance plan. Damien is currently covered under Damien's wife's health insurance policy.

Disability Insurance

Sheila has disability coverage provided through her employer (60% of gross pay coverage, own occupation, 90-day elimination period). Crescent City Publications does not provide disability insurance to its employees. Bob has purchased a disability policy on his own. The policy is own occupation that provides 65% of gross pay coverage and a 180-day elimination period. The premium for this policy is $1,200 per year, and the policy provides benefits to age 65.

Property and Liability Auto Insurance

	Bob and Sheila's cars	Angel's car
Type	PAP	PAP
Liability (Bodily injury)	$100,000/$300,000	$50,000/$100,000
Property Damage	$50,000	$25,000
Medical Payments	$1,000	$1,000
Physical Damage, own car	Actual Cash Value	Actual Cash Value
Uninsured Motorist	$100,000/$300,000	N/A
Collision Deductible	$1,000	N/A
Comprehensive Deductible	$500	N/A
Annual Premium	$1,800 (2 cars)	$1,350

Homeowners Insurance

	Personal Residence	Ski Condo
Type	HO3	HO3
Dwelling	$150,000	$150,000
Other Structures	$15,000	$15,000
Personal Property	$75,000	$75,000
Personal Liability	$100,000	$100,000
Medical Payments	$1,000	$1,000
Deductible	$250	$500
Co Insurance Clause	80/20	80/20
Annual Premium	$1,500	$1,100

Umbrella Liability Insurance

The policy coverage is for $2 million and their premium is $300 per year.

INVESTMENT INFORMATION

The Gillises have a required rate of return of 9%. They consider themselves to be moderate to moderate-aggressive investors, and they consider $50,000 an adequate amount for an emergency fund.

INCOME TAX INFORMATION

The Gillises are in the 28% marginal tax bracket for Federal income tax purposes. Capital gains are taxed at 20%. There is no state income tax.

RETIREMENT INFORMATION

Sheila is eligible to participate in her employer's 401(k) plan, but she has chosen not to participate. Her employer provides a match of dollar for dollar up to 3% of her gross salary.

Bob does not have a retirement plan at Crescent City Publications, but he usually makes IRA contributions for Sheila and himself.

Bob has several other retirement accounts from previous employers, all of which are qualified assets.

Bob and Sheila would both like to retire when Bob reaches age 65. They believe that together they would need about $75,000 (in today's dollars) pre-tax income during their retirement. This amount would decrease by 1/3 at the death of the first spouse.

Although Bob is battling cancer, they believe that his condition is not terminal and expect him to live to age 95. Sheila also expects to live to age 95.

GIFTS, ESTATES, TRUSTS, AND WILL INFORMATION

Gifts
Neither Bob nor Sheila has made any previous taxable gifts.

Estates
Bob and Sheila estimate that funeral expenses will be $25,000 and administrative expenses will be $40,000 for each of them.

Wills

Bob and Sheila both have wills, which leave $100,000 to each child with the remainder of the estate going to the surviving spouse. The wills also establish a credit equivalency trust, with all expenses and taxes to be paid from the residue of the estate.

STATEMENT OF CASH FLOWS
Bob and Sheila Gillis
Statement of Cash Flows (Expected)
For the year 1999

CASH INFLOWS

Salary - Bob	$60,000	
Salary – Sheila	28,000	
Investment Income[1]	9,508	
Rental Income	2,100	
TOTAL CASH INFLOWS		$99,608

CASH OUTFLOWS
Ordinary Living Expenses

Savings – IRA Contributions	$ 4,000	
Food	4,800	
Clothing	2,500	
Travel	3,500	
Entertainment at Home	1,500	
Utilities	3,000	
Telephone	3,600	
Auto Maintenance	2,400	
Pool Service	700	
Lawn Service	840	
Church	1,200	
Total Ordinary Living Expenses		$28,040

Other Payments

Automobile Payment	$ 7,200	
Mortgage Payment (Principal Residence)	11,747	
Mortgage Payment (Ski Condo)	12,943	
Total Other Payments		$31,890

Insurance Premiums

Automobile	$ 3,150	
Disability	1,200	
Health	0	
Homeowners	2,600	
Life	1,650	
Umbrella	300	
Total Insurance Premiums		$ 8,900

Taxes

Federal Income Tax	$22,000	
FICA-Sheila ($28,000 @ 7.65%)	2,142	
FICA-Bob ($60,000 @ 7.65%)	4,590	
Property Tax (Principal Residence)	500	
Property Tax (Ski Condo)	300	
Total Taxes		$29,532
TOTAL EXPENSES AND PLANNED SAVINGS		$98,362
BALANCE AVAILABLE FOR DISCRETIONARY INVESTMENT		$ 1,246

Notes:

[1]Investment Income:

	Checking	$ 0
	Savings	764
	Crescent City Stock	0
	Brokerage Account	1,594
	Bond Mutual Fund	* 0
	Bond Portfolio	6,250
	High Tech Stock	800
	Brown Forman Stock	100
	TOTAL	$9,508

* All income is automatically reinvested in the fund.

STATEMENT OF FINANCIAL POSITION

Bob and Sheila Gillis
Balance Sheet as of January 1, 1999

	ASSETS[1]				LIABILITIES[5,7] & NET WORTH	
	Cash & Cash Equivalents				**Current Liabilities**	
JT	Checking[2]	$8,000		H	Automobile Notes Payable	$19,000
JT	Savings[4,10]	25,475		W	Credit Cards	3,500
	Total Cash & Equivalents	$33,475			*Current Liabilities*	$22,500
	Invested Assets					
H	Stock in Crescent City				**Long-Term Liabilities**	
	Publications[3]	$160,000				
H	Brokerage Account	58,121		JT	Mortgage on Residence	$139,150
H	Bond Mutual Fund Portfolio	136,000		H	Mortgage on Ski Condo	107,627
H	Bond Portfolio	100,000			*Long-Term Liabilities*	$246,777
H	High Tech Stock[8]	20,000				
W	Brown Forman Stock[9]	5,000			*Total Liabilities*	$269,277
H	Pension Plan #1[6]	34,594				
H	Pension Plan #2[6]	98,676				
H	IRA Rollover[6]	65,078				
H	IRA-Bob	14,650				
W	IRA-Sheila	17,350				
H	Cash Value Life Insurance	5,000				
	Total Invested Assets	$714,469			**Net Worth**	$965,667
	Use Assets					
JT	Personal Residence[4]	$180,000				
H	Ski Condo	120,000				
JT	Personal Property[4]	100,000				
H	Automobiles (3)	87,000				
	Total Use Assets	$487,000			**Total Liabilities &**	
	Total Assets	$1,234,944			**Net Worth**	$1,234,944

Notes to Financial Statements:
1 Assets are stated at fair market value with exception of Crescent City Publications stock.
2 Joint tenancy with survivorship rights with son, Damien. Checking account does not earn interest. Bob contributed 100%.
3 This is Bob's guess at what Crescent City Publications is worth. His basis is $25,000.
4 Joint tenancy with survivorship rights with spouse.
5 Liabilities are stated at principal only.
6 All pension plans have the spouse of participant as named beneficiary.
7 All liabilities go with the associated asset for title purposes.
8 2,000 shares @ $10 per share. The current dividend is $0.40 per share and is expected to grow at 3% per year.
9 100 shares.
10 The current interest rate for savings accounts is 3%.

Title Designations:
H = Husband (sole owner)
W = Wife (sole owner)
JT = Joint tenancy with survivorship rights

INFORMATION REGARDING ASSETS AND LIABILITIES

HighTech Stock

This stock was given to Bob as a Christmas present after being purchased October 15, 1995 by Bob's brother Brian. Brian's basis in the HighTech Stock was $13,500, and the value at the date of the gift was $25,000. The current value of the stock is $20,000. The stock currently pays a dividend of $0.40. See Footnote on Statement of Financial Position.

Bond - Mutual Fund Portfolio of Bonds

The bond fund was inherited from Bob's uncle, Butler, who died December 10, 1997 at which time the bond fund was valued at $148,000. Uncle Butler had just bought the bond fund on November 1, 1997 and paid $145,000 for it. All earnings are automatically reinvested in the fund and Bob has had no distributions since inheriting it. The fund earned $6,000 in 1998 but unfortunately is only valued at $136,000 today due to changes in interest rates.

Bond Portfolio

Description	Maturity	Coupon[3]	Cost Basis	FMV
10,000 US T-Bills	1	N/A	$9,640.00	$9,643.20
20,000 US T-Bonds	30	8%	20,000.00	22,494.47
10,000 US T- Bonds	20	0%	1,313.00	2,625.30
20,000 Big Co. Bonds[1]	20	9%	20,000.00	24,271.01
15,000 Weak Co. Bonds[2]	25	9%	15,000.00	3,000.47
25,000 Texas Municipal Bonds	15	6%	25,000.00	27,616.29
			$90,953.00	$89,650.74
Money Market Account				$10,349.26
TOTAL				$100,000.00

Account Value as of 12/31/98: **$100,000.00**

Notes:
1 Bonds are investment quality.
2 Bonds are non-investment quality.
3 Assume all coupon payments are made once a year.

Brokerage Account

Stock[1]	Shares	Beta	Std. Dev.	Div. Yield[2]	Average Return	Cost	FMV
Big Co.	1,000	0.88	12.5%	4.0%[3]	12.5%	$8,046.47	$14,500.00
Small Co.	1,000	1.24	18.0%	0.0%	15.0%	10,724.35	12,333.00
Oil Co.	1,000	1.00	10.0%	3.5%[3]	8.0%	11,135.70	15,150.00
Auto Co.	1,000	1.12	10.0%	3.0%[4]	10.0%	12,124.72	16,138.00
					Total	$42,031.24	$58,121.00

Notes:
1 The stock portfolio has a correlation coefficient with the market of 0.80.
2 The Dividend yield is the current yield.
3 Growth of dividend is expected to remain at 3%.
4 The expected growth of the dividend is zero.

Brown Forman Stock

Sheila inherited the Brown Forman stock from her great aunt Arlene, who had bought the stock when the price was $42.00 per share. When Arlene died, she left Sheila 50 shares of Brown Forman stock. Sheila knows that on the date of Arlene's death Brown Forman stock closed at $35.00 per share with a high price of $38.00 and low price of $34.00. The stock has since split two for one and has a current dividend yield of 2%.

Personal Residence

The Gillises purchased their personal residence for $175,000 nine months ago. They put down 20% from the sale of their previous home. They were able to get a mortgage rate of 7.5% financed over 30 years. Their monthly payment is $978.90 with a balance of $139,150.39 and 351 payments remaining.

Ski Condo

Bob purchased the ski condo three years ago for $150,000 and put 20% down. The balance was financed over 15 years at 7%. The monthly payment is $1,078.59, and they have made 30 payments. The balance on the loan is $107,627.07.

Since the purchase of the condo, Bob has incurred the following restoration costs:

Wood floors	$2,000
Furniture	3,500
Ceiling Fans	300
Carpet	1,200
Kitchen appliances	2,200
Total	$9,200

The Gillises use the condo quite often in the winter and summer, but they are usually able to rent it to friends for 14 days per year at $150.00 per day.

QUESTIONS

1.   List the Gillises' financial strengths and weaknesses.

    a.   Strengths:

    b.   Weaknesses:

2.   After reading the case, what additional information would you request from the Gillises to complete your data-gathering phase?

3.   If Bob were to die today, what would be the value of his gross estate?

4.   If Bob were to die today, what would be the value of his probate assets?

5.   What would be Bob's estate tax liability if he died today, assuming Bob's last medical, funeral, and administrative expense were $65,000?

6.   Evaluate Bob's current estate plan.

7.   If Sheila were to die today, what would be the value of her gross estate?

8.   What would be the value of Sheila's probate estate if she died today?

9.   What would be Sheila's estate tax liability if she died today, assuming Sheila's last medical, funeral, and administrative expenses were $65,000?

10.   Assume Bob dies today and Sheila dies very soon thereafter. Calculate the second-to-die estate tax liability.

11.   Bob is considering selling the Mutual Fund bond portfolio and expects to receive net proceeds of $136,000 from such sale. What are the tax consequences in 1999 of such a sale assuming that it takes place on April 15, 1999?

12.   Bob is considering disposing of his stock in Crescent City Publications by
        one or more of the following methods: GRAT, Private Annuity, CRAT,
        Installment Sale (SCIN). Which one or ones are reasonable under the
        circumstances? Any sale contemplates getting the value of the stock out
        of his estate.

13.   Which assets of Bob's would be the best to gift to children if the objective
        is estate minimization?

14.   Bob is considering making a gift of 40% of Crescent City Publications to his favorite son, Damien. He discusses this transaction with a valuation expert who tells him that the company is probably worth $350,000. However, the valuation expert also says that with the transfer of 40% he could certainly apply a valuation discount of 50%. Answer the following questions assuming that Bob does make the gift with the above appraisal information.

a.   What is the value of the gift that would be reported on Form 709?

b.   Assuming Bob and Sheila decided to split the gift, how much is the taxable gift, which will be reported on Bob's Form 709?

c.   What are the requirements for making the split gift election?

d.   How much of Sheila's unified credit will remain, assuming this is her first gift?

15.   To improve Bob's estate plan you are considering how to structure the estate. Based on the facts in the case, what is the best disposition arrangement for Bob with regards to assets? (Outright bequest? A power of appointment trust? A bypass trust? A QTIP trust? A CRUT?)

16.   Assume they can earn their required rate of return, how much each do they need when Bob is age 65 to provide for both of them in retirement? (Round to the nearest thousand and assume they are both living and expected to live to 95.)

17.   Regarding planning for the Federal generation-skipping transfer tax (GSTT), describe the Gillises' situation?

18.   In recommending a bypass estate plan for the Gillises, you intend to suggest that their estate planning attorney include certain clauses in the final principal dispositive instrument, whether it turns out to be a will or a living trust. Which clause or clauses would you recommend?

19.   Which bonds in the Bond Portfolio are subject to:
       a.   Default risk?

       b.   Reinvestment rate risk?

       c.   Foreign currency risk?

       d.   Interest rate risk?

       e.   Liquidity risk?

20.   How would Bob protect his gain in Big Co. stock without selling the stock?

21.   Determine the yield to maturity for each bond using the current fair market value.

22.   Determine the duration for each bond.

23.   Based on the value of the bonds in the bond portfolio, what have interest rates been doing during the holding period?

24.   How much cash and cash equivalents do the Gillises actually have?

25.   How long have the stocks in the brokerage account been held? Assume the average rate of return in your analysis.

26.   Using the Capital Asset Pricing Model, determine the expected return for each of the stocks in the portfolio.

27.   Using Jensen's model, determine alpha for each of the stocks in the Brokerage account. Assume that the actual returns are as follows:

	Actual Return
Big Co.	13.0%
Small Co.	13.5%
Oil Co.	9.0%
Auto Co.	10.5%

28.   What is the expected return of the entire stock portfolio in terms of dollars? In percentage terms?

29.   What is the weighted alpha of the entire stock portfolio (using the actual returns in Question 27)?

30.   Assuming an income tax rate of 30%, what is the pre-tax equivalent yield to maturity for the Texas Municipal bonds?

31.   How does the return on the municipal bond compare with other interest rates?

32.   Based on other prevailing interest rates, does the pre-tax return for the Texas Municipal bond seem reasonable? Why?

33.   Determine the holding period return for each of the stocks in the Brokerage account. Ignore dividends for this purpose.

34.   What percent of the change in the value of the brokerage account can be explained by changes in the stock market?

35.   Determine the percent of the following risks that affect the Gillises' brokerage account.

       a.   Systematic risk.

       b.   Unsystematic risk.

36.   Based on the Constant Growth Dividend Model, what would the Gillises'
       required rate of return have to be for the High Tech Stock to be priced
       fairly? What are the implications on buying, selling, or holding the stock?

37.   Bob only recently made Damien the co-owner of Bob's checking account.
       What are the consequences to Bob? When does this become a taxable
       gift from Bob to Damien?

38.   Crescent City Publications used a cross purchase life insurance program
       to protect themselves from early and untimely death of a principal
       shareholder. Bob owns 80%; two other individuals (A and C) own 10%
       each. Assume that Crescent City Publications is worth $350,000. How
       many policies did they have and for what amounts?

39.   Determine the basis in Sheila's Brown Foreman stock.

40.   If Sheila were to sell the Brown Foreman stock today, what would be the income tax consequences for 1999?

41.   How much interest can the Gillises deduct from their income tax in 1999?

42.   Using the dividend growth model, determine the price per share for each
        of the following stocks:

        a.   Big Co.

        b.   Oil Co.

        c.   Auto Co.

43.   Since Bob has been diagnosed with cancer, he has been concerned
        about his health. He forgot to make his IRA contribution for 1999. Can
        he still make a 1999 contribution in 2000?

44.   Bob wants your help in determining the probability of achieving certain returns within his portfolio.

    a.   Determine the probability of getting a positive return for the Big Co.

    b.   Determine the probability of getting a return above 30% from Auto Co.

    c.   Determine the probability of earning a return between 15% and 33% for Small Co.

45.   Bob is considering re-balancing his brokerage account portfolio by selling the Oil Co. stock and the Auto Co. stock. He wants to invest the entire portfolio as follows:

- 60% in Small Co.
- 40% in Big Co.

The two stocks have a tendency to not move together since the correlation between them is only 0.3.

If Bob pays 20% tax for capital gains out of this portfolio, how much will be invested in the Big Co. and Small Co.?

46.   What is the expected return for this new portfolio? Assume the same facts as in Question 45.

47.   What will be the standard deviation of his new portfolio? Assume the same facts as in Questions 45 and 46.

48.   Bob and Sheila have the following income and expenses from the rental of the condo during 1998:

Rental Income (14 days @ $150 per day)	$2,100.00
Interest Expense	$7,733.41
Property Tax	$300.00
Depreciation	$4,800.00
Utilities	$1,000.00

How should they treat the above items on their current Federal income tax return?

49.   Bob has surgery in January 1999 to remove a small tumor from his arm and is hospitalized for several days. While in the hospital, he incurs $3,200 in expenses. How much will he have to pay (i.e., how much is not covered by the health insurance policy)?

50.   Crescent City Publications had earnings of $27,000 last year. How does
        the capitalized earnings approach method of valuation compare with
        Bob's guess of what Crescent City is worth? Use the Gillises' required
        rate of return.

51.   Based on the earnings of $27,000, how does Bob's guess of the value of
        Crescent City compare with using the P/E ratio of similar companies to
        determine the value of Crescent City? Assume the P/E ratio for similar
        companies is 12:1.

52.   If Bob sold the ski condo and all the contents in 1999 for $160,000, how
        much tax would he pay from this sale?   Assume a real estate
        commission of 6%.

USE THE FOLLOWING INFORMATION FOR QUESTIONS 53 THROUGH 57

Bob is concerned about the price of Big Co. During July 1999, he decides to buy a put option to protect his position in the stock. The price of the stock has dropped to $14.00 per share. The put option has an expiration of January 2000, and exercise price of $13.00 and a premium of $2.00.

53.   How many option contracts should he buy to fully hedge his long-position in Big Co. stock?

54.   Bob fully hedges his position with the above option. On December 31, 1998, the price of the stock has dropped $10.

   a.   What is his gain or loss on the option contracts?

   b.   How much gain or loss does he have to recognize for this put on his 1998 Form 1040?

c. How much is the gain or loss on his long position in Big Co. for the time he has held this option?

d. Based on your analysis, has Bob done an effective job of hedging Big Co. stock? If not, why? What alternative strategy might you suggest? Describe the pros and cons of the put and your suggestions, if applicable.

55. In January 2000, the option expires unexercised. The price of Big Co. has increased to $15.00 per share. How should Bob treat this on his 2000 individual tax return (Form 1040)?

56. Since the price of Big Co. stock has rebounded and the entire market is doing well, Bob believes that the price of Big Co. will continue to increase above the $15.00 level (current price). How do you advise him as his financial planner?

57.   After your discussion with him, Bob decides to enter into a futures contract on the S&P 500 to take advantage of the rising market. The contract expires January 2001.

   a.   Should he buy or sell the contract?

   b.   The S&P 500 contract has had the following prices:

          Upon entering into contract $100
          At 12/31/98 $110
          Expiration $125

          How much gain or loss should Bob report for tax purposes in 1998 and 1999? What is the nature of this gain or loss?

THIS PAGE IS INTENTIONALLY LEFT BLANK.

GEORGE AND JAN BECKER

CASE SCENARIO AND QUESTIONS

GEORGE AND JAN BECKER

Table of Contents

GEORGE AND JAN BECKER

Case Scenario and Questions

George and Jan Becker have come to you, a financial planner, for help in developing a plan to accomplish their financial goals.   Assume today is December 31, 1998 and you have gathered the following information:

PERSONAL BACKGROUND AND INFORMATION

George Becker *(Age 56)*

George owns his own business, a small jewelry store, with Schedule C Net Income of $40,000 in 1998. George's only employee is his son, Bill, who works part-time.

Jan Becker *(Age 51)*

Jan is a professor of Physics at State University where she has been employed full-time since 1980. Her W-2 income, which is $50,000 for 9 months of teaching, is paid ratably over 12 months at $4,166.67 per month.

The Beckers

George and Jan have been married for five years. Both are in excellent health. They provide some financial support to Jan's father, Ralph, who is in a nursing home. Ralph is not a dependent of the Beckers for tax purposes.

The Children

George and Jan have two children (twins), Jack and Jill (Age 5). George has two children Bill (Age 17) and Alice (Age 12) from a former marriage. Bill works part-time in the jewelry store (less than 20 hours per week).

PERSONAL AND FINANCIAL OBJECTIVES

1. The Beckers want to retire when George is 62 and Jan is 57.
2. They want to increase their tax-advantaged savings.
3. They want to be debt free of all mortgages at retirement.
4. They want to minimize their estate tax liability and avoid the costs of probate.
5. They want to transfer the jewelry business to Bill at their death or retirement.

ECONOMIC INFORMATION

They expect inflation to average 4% over the long-term. The historical return on the market has been 12% and is expected to continue. The market has had a standard deviation of 14%, which is expected to continue.

T-bills are currently yielding 3% while T-bonds are yielding 5%.

INSURANCE INFORMATION

Life Insurance

	Policy #1	Policy #2
Person Insured	George	Jan
Face Amount	$200,000	$200,000
Cash Value	$0	$0
Type of Policy	Term	Group Term
Annual Premium	$1,600	Employer paid
Beneficiary	Jan	Debra (Jan's mother)
Contingent Beneficiary	None	None
Policy Owner	George	Jan
Settlement Option Clause	Life Annuity	None Chosen

Health Insurance

Person's Covered	Family
Type of Policy	Comprehensive Basic/State University Plan
Coverage	Major Medical 80/20, $2,500 stop loss
Deductible	$500 family deductible
Annual Premiums	Employer paid

Automobile Insurance

Type	Personal Auto Policy
Liability	$100,000/$300,000/$50,000
Medical payments	$3,000/person/accident
Uninsured motorist	$50,000/accident
Physical damage, own car	Actual cash value
Collision deductible	$200
Comprehensive deductible	$50
Annual premium for 2 cars	$1,000

Homeowners Insurance

Residence	
Type	HO3 Special Form
Dwelling	$196,000
Personal property	$98,000
Personal liability	$100,000/occurance
Medical payments	$5,000/person/occurance
Deductible	$250
Premium (annual)	$1,000
Other	80/20 coinsurance clause

Condominium	
Type	HO6 Personal property
Personal liability	$300,000
Medical payments	$2,000 person/occurrence
Deductible	$500
Premium (annual)	$850
Other	$15,000 Covers renters with a rider

Disability Insurance (long-term)

Disability Policy	
Insured	Jan
Definition	Own occupation
Premium	Employer pays 60%; Jan pays 40% Total premium of $600 per year
Elimination period	90 days
Benefit	60% of gross pay (currently $2,500 per month)

Section 79 Costs For Group Term Insurance (Costs per $1,000 of protection for one month)

Age	Cost
45 through 49	$0.29
50 through 54	$0.48
55 through 59	$0.75

INCOME TAX INFORMATION

The Beckers file married filing jointly. They are in the 28% Federal marginal tax bracket. There is no state income tax.

Bill and Alice are claimed as dependents by George's former wife.

RETIREMENT INFORMATION

Savings

The Beckers currently save $15,250 annually, consisting of $4,000 contributed to their IRAs, $9,750 in reinvested dividends and interest, and $1,500 contributed to Jan's retirement plan.

Titling of Retirement Accounts	Beneficiary Designation
George's IRA	Jan
Jan's IRA	George
Jan's D/C Retirement Plan	George

Social Security Benefits

George's Social Security benefits at full retirement age of approximately 65.2 years are estimated to be $12,000 per year (in today's dollars).

Retirement Plan

State University has a mandatory defined contribution plan and contributes 7% of Jan's salary. She must contribute 3%, but the 3% is currently after-tax because of her election.

TSA 403(b) Plan

The university has a Tax Sheltered Annuity plan for Jan. She can contribute 16% (tax deductible) of her salary. Jan currently does not make use of the 403(b). The plan contains a loan provision.

GIFTS, ESTATES, TRUSTS, AND WILL INFORMATION

George's Will

George's will leaves the business and his automobile to his son Bill and everything else to his wife Jan. Jan is the executrix for the estate. The residuary legatee is to pay all administrative expenses, costs, and taxes. Any indebtedness goes with the respective asset.

Jan's Will

Jan's will leaves everything to George.

STATEMENT OF CASH FLOWS

George and Jan Becker
Statement of Cash Flows
January 1, 1998 - December 31, 1998
(Projected to be similar in 1999)

INFLOWS

George's Schedule C Net Income	$40,000	
Jan's Faculty Salary	50,000	
Dividend Income from Common Stocks	6,750	
Condo Rental Income (net of mgt fees)	12,000	
Interest Income from Bonds	3,000	
Total Inflows		**$111,750**

OUTFLOWS

Savings and Investments		$15,250
Fixed Outflows		
Alimony Payment	$ 6,000	
Mortgage Principal Residence (P&I)	19,498	
Taxes-Principal Residence	1,800	
Principal Residence Insurance	1,000	
Mortgage Condo-Rental (P&I)	14,591	
Condo Operating Costs	1,200	
Taxes-Condo	800	
Condo Association Dues	3,600	
Condo Insurance Premium	850	
Auto Note Payment	5,928	
Auto Insurance Premium	1,000	
Life Insurance Premium	1,600	
Disability Insurance Premium	240	
Total Fixed Outflows		$58,107
Variable Outflows		
Taxes	$22,945	
Food (including dining out)	4,800	
Transportation	2,600	
Clothing/Personal Care	2,800	
Entertainment/Vacations	4,000	
Medical/Dental	2,000	
Utilities & Household Expenses	2,000	
Church Donations	520	
Miscellaneous	68	
Total Variable Outflows		$41,733
Total Outflows		**$115,090**
Deficit		**($ 3,340)**

Tax Detail:	FICA George*	$ 5,652
	FICA Jan	3,825
	Fed W/H	13,468
		$22,945

*FICA: $40,000 x 15.3% x 92.35% = $5,652 (The technical calculation per Schedule SE.)

STATEMENT OF FINANCIAL POSITION

George and Jan Becker
Statement of Financial Position
As of December 31, 1998

ASSETS[1]			LIABILITIES & NET WORTH		
Cash And Cash Equivalents			**Liabilities[4]**		
Cash and checking JTWROS	$	15,000	Automobile Notes Payable JT	$	14,750
Money Market JTWROS		20,000	Mortgage Condo[2]		99,330
Total Cash And Equivalents	$	35,000	Mortgage personal residence		153,115
			Total Liabilities	$	267,195
Invested Assets					
Proprietorship H	$	400,000			
IRA-George H		40,000			
IRA-Jan W		50,000			
Common Stock Portfolio H		135,000			
Bond Portfolio W		40,000			
Rental Real Estate Condo[2]					
JTWROS		160,000			
Retirement Plan W		80,000			
TSA 403(b) Plan W		0			
Total Invested Assets	$	905,000	**Net Worth**		$1,057,805
Use Assets					
Personal Residence[3] -Dwelling	$	260,000			
& Land JTWROS		20,000			
Art Collection W		25,000			
Automobiles JT		20,000			
Personal Property JTWROS		60,000			
Total Use Assets	$	385,000			
Total Assets		$1,325,000	**Total Liabilities and Net Worth**		$1,325,000

Notes to Financial Statements:
1 Assets are stated at fair market value.
2 Condo refinanced in 1995 at 10.5%. Original balance $110,000 at December 15, 1995.
   Financed for 15 years. The first payment was due January 15, 1995.
3 Personal residence financed December 1, 1996 for $165,000 at 8.5% fixed for 15 years.
4 Liabilities are stated at principal only.

Title Designations:
H = Husband (sole owner)
W = Wife (sole owner)
JT = Joint tenancy/No survivorship
JTWROS = Joint Tenancy with Right of Survivorship

INFORMATION REGARDING ASSETS AND LIABILITIES

Proprietorship

This business was purchased by George in 1989 for $100,000. There have been no additional capital contributions.

Equity Portfolio

Mutual Fund	Shares	FMV	Basis	Beta	Standard Deviation
A	1,000	$25,000	$10,000	1.3	25%
B	2,000	$40,000	$40,000	1.0	15%
C	6,000	$60,000	$45,000	0.9	20%
D	200	$10,000	$15,000	1.2	18%

Notes to Equity Portfolio:

1. The portfolio of mutual funds has a correlation of 0.50 with the market.
2. The portfolio has had a historical return of 14% with a volatility of approximately 18%, as measured by standard deviation.

Bond Portfolio

The bond portfolio was a gift to Jan from her Uncle Mike in 1994. The value at the time of the gift was $28,000. Mike paid gift tax of $10,000 on the gift. The bonds currently earn 7.5% annually. Mike had originally paid $33,000 for the bonds.

Rental Property (condo)

This condo was purchased in January 1983 for $110,000. The depreciation method used was ACRS 15 years. The current adjusted taxable basis of the condo is $0 plus land cost of $10,000. The property is exclusively rental property.

Art Collection

The art collection was acquired from Jan's mother in 1994 as a gift. At the time of the gift, Jan's mother's basis was $5,000 while the fair market value of the collection was $30,000. Jan's mother paid gift tax of $5,000 on this gift.

Divorce Decree and Alimony

George was divorced from Susan in 1993, and he remarried the same year. His divorce decree calls for payments to his former spouse (Susan) of $500 per month for support until year 2004 at which time Alice will be 18. The payments will then be reduced to $300 per month for five more years. In the event of Susan's early death, payments are to be made to Susan's estate for the remainder of the 15-year period.

QUESTIONS

1.   List the Beckers' financial strengths and weaknesses.

    a.   Strengths:

    b.   Weaknesses:

2.   After reading the case, what additional information would you request from the Beckers to complete your data-gathering phase?

3.   What is the amount of alimony that George and Jan can deduct as alimony on their 1998 Federal Tax Return?

4.   What amount, if any, will be included in Jan's W-2 as a result of her group term insurance?

5.   What are the current insurance deficiencies of the Beckers?

6.   If Jan were to become disabled March 31, 1999 and remain disabled for the balance of 1999, how much would she collect in disability benefits during 1999?

7.   How much if any of Jan's disability benefits for 1999 would be taxable if she were to become disabled March 31, 1999 and remained disabled for the balance of the year?

8.   If the Beckers were to have a fire in their personal residence, which resulted in a loss of $20,000, how much of the loss would be paid by the insurance company?

9.   If Jan were to sell the bond portfolio today for the value on the Statement of Financial Position, what would be the tax consequences for 1999?

10. What is Jan's adjusted tax basis in the art collection?

11. Discuss the investment characteristics of the art collection and its valuation.

12. Assume the Beckers make a $4,000 contribution ($2,000 each) to traditional IRA accounts in 1999. What is the amount of their deductible IRA contributions for 1999?

13.   What is the approximate tax liability for the Beckers for 1998?

14.   What kind of retirement plan would allow George the greatest deductible contribution while providing him with only a small cash flow commitment each year? What would be the maximum percentage contribution for a person like George?

15.   If the alimony is not deductible, how long do George and Susan have to amend their divorce decree to make the alimony deductible?

16.   Calculate the estimated tax liability for 1999 for the Beckers. Assume
       that George maximizes any pension contribution and that Jan maximizes
       her tax benefits from retirement and 403(b) contribution. Also assume
       that the alimony is deductible.

17.   How would their savings change as a result of the pension plan for him
       and the 403(b) plan for her?

18.   What are the characteristics of a TSA?

19.   What amount of Social Security benefits can George collect at age 62?

20.   Discuss the pros and cons of George establishing the following retirement plans:

     a.   SEP.

     b.   15% Profit Sharing Plan.

     c.   25% Money Purchase Plan.

     d.   10% Money Purchase and 15% Profit Sharing Plan.

21.   If George were to die today, what is the value of his gross estate?

22.   If George were to die today, what is the value of his probate assets?

23.   Assume George's last medical, funeral, and administrative expense were $50,000. What is George's estate tax liability if he died today?

24.   Evaluate George's current estate plan.

25.   If Jan were to die today, what is the value of her gross estate?

26.   What is the value of Jan's probate assets if she died today?

27. Assume Jan's last medical, funeral, and administrative expenses were $50,000. What is Jan's estate tax liability if she died today?

28. Evaluate Jan's current estate plan.

29. Assume George dies today and Jan dies very soon thereafter. Calculate the second to die estate tax liability.

30.   Evaluate the current overall estate plan.

31.   What devices could be used to avoid the poor results of Question 30?

BYRON AND NANCY MELANCON

CASE SCENARIO AND QUESTIONS

BYRON AND NANCY MELANCON
Table of Contents

BYRON AND NANCY MELANCON

Case Scenario and Questions

Today is January 1, 1999. Byron and Nancy Melancon have come to you, a financial planner, for help in developing a plan to accomplish their financial goals. From your initial meeting together, you have gathered the following information:

PERSONAL BACKGROUND AND INFORMATION

Byron Melancon (Age 61)

Byron has been employed 25 years as a Vice President for an oil field services company. He participates in a defined benefit plan. Byron's first wife died.

Nancy Melancon (Age 29)

Nancy owns Publications, Inc. and Nancy's Advertising, Inc.

The Melancons

They met July 4, 1996 at a fourth of July picnic. Byron was rollerblading and had a nasty fall. Nancy saw him fall and ran to his rescue. She drove him to the emergency room and that is where they fell in love. They have been together ever since and married in November of the same year. They have no children together.

Byron's Children

Byron has four children from his first marriage:

Martin	Age 34
Julius	Age 33
Brad	Age 32
Laena	Age 31

All of the children are healthy, employed, married, and not living with Byron and Nancy.

PERSONAL AND FINANCIAL OBJECTIVES

- Nancy plans to sell her businesses.
- Byron plans to retire in 1999 (January 1, 1999) (his life expectancy is 25.75 years).
- Nancy's life expectancy is 57.75 years and that is also the joint life expectancy.
- They plan to sell their primary residence.
- They plan to refinance their vacation home.
- They plan to travel extensively before deciding where to permanently relocate.

ECONOMIC INFORMATION

- They expect inflation to average 3% (CPI) annually over both the short and the long-term.
- They expect stock market returns of 11% annually on the S&P 500 Index.
- T-Bills are currently yielding 5%.
- Current mortgage rates are:

  Fixed 15-year   6.75%

  Fixed 30-year   7.25%
- Mortgage closing costs are expected to be 3% of any mortgage.
- They will finance all closing costs in any refinance.

INSURANCE INFORMATION

Life Insurance

	Policy 1	Policy 2
Insured	Byron	Nancy
Owner	Byron	Nancy
Beneficiary	Children	Byron
Face Amount	$150,000	$150,000
Cash Value	$0	$0
Type of Policy	Term	Term
Settlement Options	Lump Sum	Lump Sum
Premium (annual)	$450	$150

Note: These are not employer provided

Health Insurance

Byron's employer currently provides health insurance for both Byron and Nancy. The employer will continue to provide the health insurance during retirement.

Disability Insurance

Neither Byron nor Nancy has disability insurance.

Homeowners Insurance

They have HO3 policies on both the primary residence and the vacation home.

	Residence	Vacation Home
Dwelling	$200,000	$150,000
Co-Insurance	80/20	80/20
Deductible	$500	$500

Umbrella Policy

They have a $3 million umbrella liability policy.

Automobile Insurance

They carry the maximum liability coverage but have no comprehensive or collision coverage.

INVESTMENT INFORMATION

- Emergency fund is adequate at $20,000.
- They can accept moderate risk.
- Byron's IRA investment portfolio is $200,000 with $100,000 invested in low to medium risk equity mutual funds. Nancy is the beneficiary of the IRA.
- The other $100,000 of the IRA is invested in staggered maturity short-term Treasury notes.
- Byron expects to use the income and some of the principal from the $100,000 to make up any shortfall between his retirement needs and his defined benefit plan annuity for the period of time until Social Security benefits are received (one year at age 62).
- Byron is currently earning 6.5% on the $100,000 invested in Treasury notes and expects the earnings rate to continue until the notes mature.

INCOME TAX INFORMATION

(See also Assets)

Byron and Nancy file a joint Federal tax return and are both average and marginal 28% Federal income taxpayers but pay no state income tax.

RETIREMENT INFORMATION

Byron (Date of birth December 31, 1937)

- Has an employer provided defined benefit plan that will pay him a joint and survivor annuity equal to 80% of single life annuity at any retirement age of 60 or later. There is no reduction for retirement at age 60 or later.
- The defined benefit formula is 1.25% times the number of years of service times the last salary with no offset for Social Security (Byron's final salary for 1998 was $100,000).

- The present value of Byron's projected annual Social Security benefits at age 66 is $13,500 per year or 80% of that amount at age 62. Social Security benefits are expected to increase proportionally with the general inflation rate.
- Byron is expected to retire immediately, January 1, 1999. He has three options to elect regarding his Defined Benefit plan assets:
    1. Take a lump sum of $400,000.
    2. Take a single life annuity beginning January 1, 1999.
    3. Take a joint and survivor annuity beginning January 1, 1999.

GIFTS, ESTATES, TRUSTS, AND WILL INFORMATION

Gifts

The following are all of the lifetime taxable gifts made.

1. In 1988, Byron gifted $200,000 to each of his four children. The $800,000 was put into an irrevocable trust. During the same year he gave $10,000 to each child (total $40,000) to use the 1988 annual exclusion. He paid gift tax of $78,000 at the time. He inherited the $918,000 ($800,000 + $40,000 + $78,000) as the primary legatee of his mother in 1988. The successor legatees were the four grandchildren (children of Byron).
2. In 1996, just before his marriage to Nancy, Byron gave each of his four children $60,000 ($50,000 taxable and $10,000 annual exclusion) and paid gift tax of $75,000 at that time.
3. Nancy has made no taxable gifts during her lifetime.

Estates

For purposes of estimating the estate tax liability (of either spouse):

- Last illness and funeral expenses are estimated to be $20,000.
- Estate administration expenses are estimated to be $30,000.

Wills

Byron and Nancy have simple wills leaving all probate assets to the other. The debts and taxes are to be paid from the inheritance of the surviving spouse.

STATEMENT OF FINANCIAL POSITION

Byron and Nancy Melancon
Statement of Financial Position
As of January 1, 1999

ASSETS[1]

Cash/Cash Equivalents

JT	Cash (Money Market)	$	40,000
	Total Cash/Cash Equivalents	$	40,000

Invested Assets

WS	Publications, Inc.	$ 300,000
WS	Nancy's Advertising, Inc.	100,000
WS	Nancy's Investment Portfolio (see detail)	90,000
HS	SPDA	110,801
HS	Byron's Investment Portfolio (IRA)	200,000
HS	Defined Benefit Plan (Vested)	400,000
	Total Investments	$1,200,801

Personal Use Assets

JT	Primary Residence	300,000
JT	Vacation Home	180,000
JT	Personal Property & Furniture	100,000
HS	Auto1	20,000
WS	Auto2	22,000
	Total Personal Use	$ 622,000
	Total Assets	**$1,862,801**

LIABILITIES AND NET WORTH[2]

Liabilities

Current:

HS	Credit Card 1	$	5,000
WS	Credit Card 2		7,000
WS	Credit Card 3		8,000
HS	Auto$_1$ Balance		10,000
WS	Auto$_2$ Balance		10,000
	Current Liabilities	$	40,000

Long-term:

Mortgage - Primary	$	150,000
Mortgage - Vacation		120,000
Long-term Liabilities	$	270,000

Total Liabilities	310,000

Net Worth	**$1,552,801**

Total Liabilities & Net Worth	**$1,862,801**

Notes to financial statements:
1 All assets are stated at fair market value.
2 Liabilities are stated at principal only.

Titles and Ownership Information
HS = Husband separate property
WS = Wife separate property
JT = Joint husband and wife (with survivorship rights)

INFORMATION REGARDING ASSETS AND LIABILITIES

Publications, Inc. (Nancy 100% shareholder of C Corporation.)

- The fair market value is $300,000.

- The original and present adjusted taxable basis is $75,000 (acquired by purchase January 1,1993).

- Nancy has agreed to sell the company for $300,000 on April 1, 1999. The terms are 20% down on April 1st, and the balance paid in equal monthly installments over 10 years at 11% interest beginning on May 1, 1999.

Nancy's Advertising, Inc. (Nancy 100% shareholder of C Corporation - Section 1244 stock.)

- She started the business January 1, 1990, and her adjusted taxable basis is $250,000.

Byron's SPDA (Single Premium Deferred Annuity)

- The SPDA was acquired December 31, 1981 for $25,000. Current fair market value is $110,801.

- Contract had back end surrender charges of 5% for the first seven years.

- Currently the earnings rate is 6% compounded quarterly.

- The annuity start date is October 1, 1999 and will consist of quarterly payments over Byron's life (Byron's life expectancy is 25 years as of October 1, 1999).

- Nancy is the named beneficiary if Byron dies before the annuity start date.

Defined Benefit Plan

- The vested benefits are valued at $400,000.

- In the event of Byron's death before retirement benefits begin, the entire balance ($400,000) is paid directly to Nancy as his named beneficiary.

Primary Residence

- The house was originally owned by Byron, but one-half was given to Nancy when they were married in 1996.
- The fair market value is $300,000 with cost basis of $140,000.
- They expect to pay 6% real estate commission on any sale of the personal residence.

Vacation Home

- The fair market value is $180,000.
- The original mortgage was for a period of 15 years at 9%.
- The original and current payment is $1,522 per month (principal and interest).
- The current mortgage balance is $120,000, with a remaining term of 120-months.

IRA Investments

- The beneficiary of Byron's IRA is Nancy.

Nancy's Detailed Investment Portfolio

Description	Qty.	FMV	Beta	Maturity	Coupon	Yearly Returns				
						98	97	96	95	94
Best Buy	200	$ 6,000.00	1.15			10%	15%	12%	6%	(5%)
Texaco	500	$10,000.00	0.90			5%	6%	3%	7%	(6%)
Kroger	1,250	$10,000.00	0.85			5%	9%	8%	8%	(1%)
Intel	400	$20,000.00	1.20			11%	15%	12%	10%	3%
Growth Fund	1,400	$21,000.00	1.15			5%	11%	14%	9%	2%
Treasury A (1 Bond)	1	$ 929.64		2	50					
Treasury B (2 Bonds)	2	$ 2,050.62		3	100					
Treasury C (2 Bonds)	2	$ 2,272.28		5	125					
Cash		$17,747.46								
Total		$90,000.00								

Note: The correlation coefficient between Nancy's portfolio and the market is 0.9

All bonds have a par value of $1,000.

QUESTIONS

1.   List the Melancons' financial strengths and weaknesses.

a.   Strengths:

b.   Weaknesses:

2.   After reading the case, what additional information would you request
from the Melancons to complete your data-gathering phase?

3.   Calculate the following financial ratios for the Melancons.

$$\frac{\text{Net Worth}}{\text{Total Assets}} \qquad =$$

$$\frac{\text{Total Debt}}{\text{Total Assets}} \qquad =$$

4.   Comment on any of the above ratios that you think are important.

5.   Excluding the down payment, what is the total of the expected installment payments to be received in 1999 by Nancy from the sale of Publications, Inc. (round to nearest dollar)?

6.   Calculate the first annuity payment from the SPDA for Byron, assuming he starts the annuity as scheduled (October 1, 1999).

7.   Byron and Nancy have decided to refinance their vacation home over the remaining life of their existing current mortgage. What will be the monthly principal and interest payment necessary to do so assuming they refinance?

8.   Assuming Byron and Nancy sell their primary residence for the fair market value today, what are their 1999 tax consequences, assuming they do not plan to reinvest for three or four years?

9.   Byron is contemplating gifting his life insurance policy to his children, who are the current beneficiaries. What is the valuation of the policy for gift tax purposes of such a gift?

10.   In the event of a $25,000 loss due to fire on the personal residence, how much will the homeowners insurance company pay of such a loss?

11.   You review the insurance coverage on Nancy and Byron for catastrophic coverage and estate planning. Discuss any deficiencies in the insurance arrangement considering catastrophic coverage and estate planning.

12.   What are the weighted beta and the weighted geometric average return of Nancy's investment portfolio over the last five years based on current market values (excluding bonds and cash)?

13.   What risks should Nancy be concerned about with regard to her investment portfolio?

14.   Considering Nancy's current Bond Portfolio, what types of risks is she not subject to, if she holds the bonds to maturity?

15.   Determine which of the following bonds Nancy should purchase if she
        wants to increase the duration of her bond portfolio.

        a.   Bond 1: Three year zero coupon bond selling for $772.18
                (Duration = 3 years).

        b.   Bond 2: Four year bond selling for $1,923.32 with an annual
                coupon of $375 (Duration = 2.985 years).

        c.   Bond 3: Four year bond selling for $983.80 with an annual
                coupon of $85 (Duration = 3.55 years).

        Note: All bonds have a maturity of $1,000.

16.   Is Nancy's portfolio of common stocks (including the mutual fund) subject
        to unsystematic risk?

17.   Using the Capital Asset Pricing Model and assuming that the market had yielded an annual compound return of 7.4% over the past five years, has Nancy's portfolio outperformed the expected return?

18.   Using the Treynor performance measure, which of the common stocks (including the mutual fund) has the best risk-adjusted return of the five securities (use the geometric average return over the five year period)?

19.   What is the tax treatment for 1999 of the down payment made on April 1, 1999 when Nancy sells Publications, Inc., assuming that she treats the sale as an installment sale?

20.   Calculate the amount of ordinary income and capital gain that Nancy will have in 1999 from the sale of Publications, Inc. (round to the nearest dollar).

21.   Assume that Nancy immediately sells Nancy's Advertising, Inc. for the current fair market value. What is the impact of such a transaction on the joint tax return for the Melancons for 1999?

22.   Assume Byron decides to withdraw $15,000 from his SPDA today, January 1, 1999. The insurance company has informed him that his quarterly annuity (ordinary) payment will be reduced to $1,911.81 per quarter. What is the income tax effect of Byron's proposed withdrawal?

23.   Assume that Byron begins his SPDA annuity as scheduled. What is the portion of that annuity that is includible in taxable income in 1999?

24.   Calculate Byron's expected Defined Benefit monthly annuity payment assuming he elects the single life annuity (round to the nearest dollar).

25.   If Byron elects to take a lump sum distribution instead of electing an annuity, what options are available to him?

26. Calculate the annual implicit earnings rate for the single and joint life annuity payments for the defined benefit plan.

27. Byron elects to take the lump sum. He believes that his after tax earnings rate on such a portfolio would be 10% and that inflation would be equal to his projected CPI. What real amount of a single life monthly annuity could he create assuming the payments were made at the beginning of each month and beginning today? What would be the nominal payment at 10%? Should he take one of the annuities or the lump sum?

28. Assuming Byron decides to take Social Security retirement benefits beginning January 1, 1999, calculate his expected annual Social Security benefits for 1999 (round to the nearest dollar).

29.   Assuming that Mr. Melancon were to die today, what is the total of his probate estate?

30.   Assuming that Mr. Melancon was to die today, what is the total of his gross estate?

31.   What would be Mr. Melancon's tentative tax base?

32. Assuming no state credits and no state estate taxes, what would Mr. Melancon's estate tax liability be?

33. What could Mr. Melancon have done back in 1988 to avoid the current estate situation and still have achieved the same result as what he accomplished with his initial gifting?

THIS PAGE IS INTENTIONALLY LEFT BLANK.

WALLACE AND KITTY REMINGTON

CASE SCENARIO AND QUESTIONS

WALLACE AND KITTY REMINGTON

Table of Contents

WALLACE AND KITTY REMINGTON

Case Scenario and Questions

Today's date is January 1, 1999. Wallace and Kitty Remington have come to you, a financial planner, for help in developing a plan to accomplish their financial goals. From your initial meeting together, you have gathered the following information:

PERSONAL BACKGROUND AND INFORMATION

Wallace Remington *(Age 65)*

Wallace Remington's date of birth is May 11, 1933. He was employed for 20 years as a partner at Remington Securities (Remington). He participates in a Keogh Plan at Remington. He was previously employed for 20 years as a broker with Smith Brothers, Inc. where he participated in a 401(k) plan.

Kitty Remington *(Age 65)*

Kitty Remington's date of birth is January 10, 1933. She has volunteered at Children's Hospital and the American Red Cross for the past 15 years.

The Remingtons

They have been married 42 years. Both Wallace and his wife, Kitty, are currently in good health, although Wallace had a mild heart attack eight years ago. Wallace's life expectancy is 17 years. Kitty's life expectancy is 20 years. Their joint life expectancy is 26 years. (Life expectancies are from Tables V and VI of Treas. Reg. 1.72-9.)

Children

		Grandchildren
Pam	Age 39	2 children
Elise	Age 36	5 children
Jackie	Age 30	4 children
Vicki	Age 29	3 children
Wallace, Jr.	Age 18	No children

All of the girls are healthy, employed, married, and not living with Wallace and Kitty. Wallace, Jr. is unemployed, single, a high school graduate, and lives with his parents.

PERSONAL AND FINANCIAL OBJECTIVES

- Wallace plans to sell his share of the business. He wants to sell half of his share of the business to his key employee, Bob Newhart. He wants to sell the other half to his oldest daughter, Pam, who is the senior broker in the firm.

- Wallace plans to retire now and begin his retirement by traveling around the world with his wife.

- After traveling around the world, Wallace plans to return to the business as a self-employed consultant on a fee basis beginning January 1, 2000.

- Wallace, Jr. will be starting at Private University in the Fall of 1999.

- Wallace's grandchild Greg, Pam's youngest child, was born with a serious physical disability. Wallace plans to give Greg $2,000,000 in a trust for his care and benefit.

ECONOMIC INFORMATION

- The couple expects inflation to average 4% annually.
- The expected stock market returns are 10% annually, as measured by the S&P 500 Index, with a standard deviation of 10%.
- Tuition is currently $30,000 per year at Private University.
- The expected education inflation rate is 5%.
- The 30-day T-bill is yielding 3.5%.
- The 30-year Treasury Bond is yielding 7.5%.
- Current mortgage rates are 7.5% for 15 years and 8.0% for 30 years. In addition, closing costs (3% of the mortgage) will be added to any refinancing loan.

INSURANCE INFORMATION

Life Insurance

Neither spouse has life insurance.

Health Insurance

Wallace's business provides health coverage for both Kitty and himself during employment and during retirement.

- Major medical 80/20.
- $250 deductible per person.
- $1,000,000 cap.
- $2,000 family stop/loss provision.

Disability insurance

Neither Wallace nor Kitty has disability insurance.

Homeowner's Insurance

They have HO3 policies on the primary residence and vacation homes.

	Residence	Vacation Home 1	Vacation Home 2
Dwelling	$975,000	$700,000	$600,000
Co-Insurance	80/20	80/20	80/20
Deductible	$250	$250	$250

Umbrella Liability Policy

$5 million of coverage

Automobile Insurance

They have the maximum liability coverage, $100,000/$300,000/$50,000, but carry no comprehensive or collision on autos.

Insurance Premiums

- Car insurance: $6,000 per year for all three of Wallace and Kitty's automobiles.
- Homeowner's insurance: $2,400 per year (includes all homes).
- Boat Insurance: $1,200 per year (covered under the umbrella policy).
- Umbrella Policy: $1,000 per year.

INVESTMENT INFORMATION

- The Remingtons have a required rate of return of 8%.

- The couple can tolerate medium to high amounts of risk, but have little need to take excessive risks due to their net worth.

- Wallace's 401(k) plan investments are secure in a well-diversified but relatively volatile group of small cap technology stocks. The funds in his 401(k) plan are still in Smith Brother's Retirement Plan.

- Wallace has a deferred single premium annuity that was purchased in 1976 (July 1st) for $60,000 and is currently worth $233,047. The expected return over the next year and the 15 years of the fixed term of the annuity is 6%. The start date of the monthly annuity is January 1, 2000, when the expected fair market value will be $247,030.

- Wallace plans to sell 4,468 shares of K-Mart stock to his daughter, Vicki, who is employed by K-Mart. Wallace anticipates the stock will greatly appreciate in the upcoming years. (The stock was purchased in 1993 for $26.66 per share and is currently trading for $11.25 per share.)

INCOME TAX INFORMATION

- Wallace and Kitty are currently in the highest Federal income tax bracket (39.6% marginal rate).

- They also pay state taxes of 5.4% for a total of 45%.

- For personal income tax reporting, Wallace has a $700,000 salary.

- They do not reside in a community property state.

RETIREMENT INFORMATION

- The 401(k) plan has a plan balance of $600,000 consisting of a portfolio of small cap value stocks. The portfolio is projected to average a return of 16% over the next 20 years with a standard deviation of 8%.

- His anticipated Social Security retirement benefit is $15,000 per year in 1999 and will increase at the expected CPI of 4%.

- He has a profit-sharing type of Keogh plan. His company contributes $12,000 per year to the profit-sharing plan. The contributions to this plan have been made out of company's profits. The balance is a result of an annual contribution of $12,000, with a 7% approximate average return since July 1, 1980.

- Wallace and Kitty will continue to collect $200,000 per year in rental proceeds from Commercial Property A.

- Wallace and Kitty will receive $50,000 per year from the Charitable Remainder Annuity Trust that owns Commercial Property B.

GIFTS, ESTATES, TRUSTS, AND WILL INFORMATION

Gifts

The following are the Remingtons' only lifetime gifts.

1. In December 1997, Wallace transferred $3,000,000 of property to a GRAT (Grantor Retained Annuity Trust). Wallace hoped to save on gift and estate taxes by transferring this portion of his interest into a trust while retaining the right to a fixed ordinary annuity for a term of 10 years. He transferred this $3,000,000 interest and kept the right to receive $298,059 per year for 10 years. The Remingtons' five children are the remainder beneficiaries of the GRAT. Upon the death of a remainderman, the interest shall pass to the remainderman's descendants. If a remainderman dies without heirs, then the remainderman's interest shall pass to the other children (remaindermen) pro rata. He paid gift tax of $153,000 in 1998. This was his first taxable transfer. Because the Section 7520 rate was 8%, the taxable gift was $1,000,000.

2. In 1997, Wallace gave each of his five children $50,000 ($40,000 taxable and $10,000 annual exclusion) and paid gift tax of $82,000 in 1998.

3. Kitty has made no taxable gifts during her lifetime nor have any gifts been split.

4. A 5% CRAT (Charitable Remainder Annuity Trust) was established by Wallace in 1998 by donating a piece of real estate (an apartment building, Commercial Property B) inherited from his grandfather. The initial valuation of the trust was $1,000,000, with the initial income in the first year projected to be $50,000 beginning in 1999. The charitable remainder beneficiary is the Chicago Art Institute. (**Note:** See excerpt from the trust document.)

5. He plans to donate $2,000,000 to an irrevocable trust for his grandchild Greg, the youngest child of Pam.

Estates

For the purpose of estimating estate tax liability of both spouses:

1. The last illness and funeral expenses are expected to be $250,000 each. (Terminal illness involved.)

2. Estate administration expenses are estimated at $200,000 each.

Wills

Mr. and Mrs. Remington have simple wills. They have left all probate assets to each other. Each will also includes a six-month survivorship clause. Debts and taxes are to be paid from the residue of the estate.

CHARITABLE REMAINDER ANNUITY TRUST

Excerpt from Wallace's Inter Vivos Charitable Remainder Annuity Trust

On this 1st day of September, 1998, I, Wallace Remington, Sr. (hereinafter referred to as "the Donor"), desiring to establish a charitable remainder annuity trust, within the meaning of section 5 of Rev. Proc. 90-32 and section 664(d)(1) of the Internal Revenue Code (hereinafter referred to as "the Code") hereby create the Remington Charitable Remainder Annuity Trust and designate James Walters, attorney at law, as the initial Trustee.

1. Funding of Trust. The Donor transfers to the Trustee the property described in Schedule A[1], and the Trustee accepts such property and agrees to hold, manage, and distribute such property of the Trust under the terms set forth in this Trust instrument.
2. Payment of Annuity Amount. In each taxable year of the Trust, the Trustee shall pay to Wallace Remington, Sr. (hereinafter known as "the beneficiary"), an annuity amount equal to 5% of the net fair market value of the assets of the Trust as of the date of this Trust. The annuity amount shall be paid in equal quarterly amounts from income and, to the extent that income is not sufficient, from principal. Any income of the Trust for a taxable year in excess of the annuity amount shall be added to principal. If the net fair market value of the Trust assets is incorrectly determined, then within a reasonable period after the value is finally determined for Federal tax purposes, the Trustee shall pay to the Charity (in the case of an undervaluation) or receive from the Charity (in the case of an overvaluation) an amount equal to the difference between the annuity amount(s) properly payable and the annuity amount(s) actually paid.
3. Upon the death of the beneficiary, the property in the trust will pass to the Chicago Art Institute (hereinafter known as "the charity").
4. If the Charitable Organization is not an organization described in sections 170(c), 2055(a), and 2522(a) of the Code at the time when any principal or income of the Trust is to be distributed to it, then the Trustee shall distribute such principal or income to such one or more organizations described in sections 170(c), 2055(a), and 2522(a) as the Trustee shall select in its sole discretion.
5. Additional Contributions. No additional contributions shall be made to the Trust after the initial contribution.
6. Prohibited Transactions. The Trustee shall make distributions at such time and in such manner as not to subject the Trust to tax under section 4942 of the Code. Except for the payment of the annuity amount to the Recipients, the Trustee shall not engage in any act of self-dealing and shall not make any taxable expenditures. The Trustee shall not make any investments that jeopardize the charitable purpose of the Trust, within the meaning of section 4944 and the regulations thereunder, or retain any excess business holdings, within the meaning of section 4943(c).
7. Taxable Year. The taxable year of the Trust shall be the calendar year.
8. Governing Law. The operation of the Trust shall be governed by the laws of the State of Illinois. The Trustee, however, is prohibited from exercising any power or discretion granted under said laws that would be inconsistent with the qualification of the Trust under section 664(d)(1) of the Code and the corresponding regulations.
9. Limited Power of Amendment. The Trust is irrevocable. The Trustee, however, shall have the power, acting alone, to amend the Trust in any manner required for the sole purpose of ensuring that the Trust qualifies and continues to qualify as a charitable remainder annuity trust within the meaning of section (1) of the Code.
10. Investment of Trust Assets. Nothing in this Trust instrument shall be construed to restrict the Trustee from investing the Trust assets in a manner that could result in the annual realization of a reasonable amount of income or gain from the sale or disposition of Trust assets.

---

[1] Schedule A simply describes the property known as Commercial Property B.

WILL

Excerpts from Wallace Remington's Statutory Last Will and Testament

I, WALLACE REMINGTON, SR. being of sound mind and wishing to make proper disposition of my property in the event of my death, do declare this to be my Last Will and Testament. I revoke all of my prior wills and codicils.

1.1   I have been married but once, and only to Kitty Remington with whom I am presently living.

1.2   Out of my marriage to Kitty Remington, five children were born namely Pam Remington, Elise Remington, Jackie Remington, Vicki Remington, and Wallace Remington, Jr.

1.3   I have adopted no one nor has anyone adopted me.

3.1   I give my entire estate to Kitty Remington, my wife.

3.2   In the event that Kitty Remington predeceases me or fails to survive me for more than six (6) months from the date of my death, I give my entire estate to my children Pam Remington, Elise Remington, Jackie Remington, Vicki Remington, and Wallace Remington, Jr. in equal and undivided 1/5 shares.

3.3   In the event that any of the named heirs or legatees should predecease me, die within six months from the date of my death, disclaim or otherwise fail to accept any property bequeath to him or her and said legatee has no descendants, his or her share of all of my property of which I die possessed shall be given to the surviving named legatees.

5.1   I name, Kitty Remington to serve as my executrix of my succession, with full seisin and without bond.

5.2   I direct that the expenses of my last illness, funeral and the administration of my estate shall be paid by my executrix as soon as practicable after my death.

5.3   All inheritance, estate, succession, transfer and other taxes (including interest and penalties thereon) payable by reason of my death shall be apportioned in accordance with the law.

STATEMENT OF CASH FLOWS

Wallace & Kitty Remington
Annual Statement of Cash Flows
January 1, 1998 - December 31, 1998

CASH INFLOWS:

Salary:	Wallace's Salary	$700,000	
	Kitty's Salary	0	
	Total Salary		$700,000
Rental Income:			200,000
Dividend Income:	Wallace	$ 5,000	
	Kitty	1,500	
	Total Dividend Income		6,500
Interest Income[1]:			1,000
Total Income:			**$907,500**

CASH OUTFLOWS:

Mortgage Payments:	Primary Residence	$ 37,030	
	Vacation Home I	45,181	
	Vacation Home II	79,308	
	Total Mortgage Payments		$161,519
Insurance Premiums:	Home Owners	$ 2,400	
	Auto	6,000	
	Boat	1,200	
	Umbrella	1,000	
	Total Insurance Premiums		$ 10,600
Misc. Expenses:	Credit Card payments	$ 2,400	
	Entertainment	50,000	
	Food	14,400	
	Clothes	30,000	
	Utilities	24,000	
	Charity	90,000	
	Total Misc. Expenses		$210,800
Tax:	Property Tax	$ 84,000	
	Income Tax	408,375	
	Total Tax		$492,375
Total Outflows:			**$875,294**
Discretionary Cash			**$ 32,206**

Notes to Financial Statements:

1 Initial income from the CRAT of $50,000 and GRAT of $298,059 is projected for January 1, 1999 ('98 payment) and was omitted from the 1998 Statement of Cash Flows.

STATEMENT OF FINANCIAL POSITION

Wallace & Kitty Remington
Statement of Financial Position
As of January 1, 1999

ASSETS [1]

Cash/Cash Equivalents		
JT	Cash	$ 100,000
Total Cash/Cash Equiv.		**$ 100,000**

Invested Assets		
JT	Remington Securities	$ 5,000,000
W	Kitty's Portfolio	500,000
H	Deferred Annuity	233,047
H	401(k) Plan	600,000
H	Keogh	526,382
H	Wallace's Portfolio	4,000,000
JT	Commercial Property A	1,500,000
Total Investments		**$12,359,429**

Personal Use Assets		
JT	Primary Residence	$ 1,300,000
JT	Vacation Home 1	800,000
JT	Vacation Home 2	700,000
JT	Personal Property/Furniture	875,000
H	Auto 1	80,000
H	Auto 2	55,000
W	Auto 3	40,000
W	Yacht	110,000
Total Personal Use		**$ 3,960,000**

Total Assets		**$16,419,429**

LIABILITIES AND NET WORTH

Liabilities[2]

Current Liabilities		
W	Credit card 1	$ 1,000
W	Credit card 2	15,000
Total Current		**$ 16,000**

Long-Term Liabilities		
JT	Mortgage - Primary	$ 258,630
JT	Mortgage - vacation 1	369,428
JT	Mortgage - vacation 2	687,444
Total Long-Term Liabilities		**$ 1,315,502**
Total Liabilities		**$ 1,331,502**

Net Worth		**$15,087,927**

Total Liabilities and Net Worth		**$16,419,429**

Notes to Financial Statements:
1 Assets are stated at fair market value (rounded to even dollars).
2 Liabilities are stated at principal only (rounded to even dollars).

Property Ownership:
JT - Joint tenancy with right of survivorship
H - Husband separate.
W - Wife separate.

INFORMATION REGARDING ASSETS AND LIABILITIES

Remington Security Investments (Wallace is a 50% partner)

- The fair market value of Wallace's interest is $5,000,000.
- The current adjusted taxable basis is $1,000,000.
- Details of the transfer of the business (Sale).
  - 50%: a 10-year installment sale to Bob Newhart for a down payment of 20% on January 1, 1999 and monthly payments beginning February 1, 1999 at 10% annual interest.
  - 50%: SCIN or private annuity to Pam.

Primary Residence

- Purchased in 1984.
- Joint-owned (JTWROS).
- Market value $1,300,000.
- Original purchase price $300,000.
- Current mortgage @ 12% interest. Payment: $3,085.84 (30 yr.) per month.

Vacation Home 1

- Joint-owned - Purchased in 1997.
- Market value $800,000.
- Original purchase price $400,000.
- Current mortgage @ 7.75% Payment: $3,765.10 (15 yr.) per month.

Vacation Home 2

- Joint-owned – Purchased in 1998.
- Market value $700,000.
- Original purchase price $700,000.
- Current mortgage @ 7.8% Payment: $6,608.99 (15 yr.) per month.

Commercial Property A

- Original site of the business.
- Fair market value: $1,500,000.
- Adjusted basis $200,000.

Single Premium Deferred Annuity

- Wallace purchased this annuity on July 1, 1978 for $60,000. The current fair market value is $233,047.
- Earning rate of 6% compounded annually is expected in near term.
- Annuity start date is January 1, 2000 at which time the fair market value is projected to be $247,030 and will consist of 180 monthly payments (15 years).
- If Wallace dies before the annuity start date, Kitty is named beneficiary (100% Joint and Survivor Annuity).

Summary of Indebtedness

Asset	Date 1st Payment	Amount of Mortgage	Term/ Years	Interest	Monthly Payments	Remaining Payments	Remaining Balance
Primary Residence	4/1/84	$300,000	30	12.00%	($3,085.84)	183	$ 258,629.70
Vacation Home 1	1/1/97	$400,000	15	7.75%	($3,765.10)	156	$ 369,427.86
Vacation Home 2	7/1/98	$700,000	15	7.80%	($6,608.99)	174	$ 687,443.56
							$1,315,501.12

Detailed Investment Portfolios

Wallace's Portfolio

Description	Acquired	Shares	Adjusted Basis	Beta	Current FMV
Sears	8/91	16,325	$201,633	0.9	$ 830,214
K-Mart	1/94	4,468	$119,117	1.2	$ 50,265
Canon Inc.	2/96	22,249	$400,188	1.4	$2,230,462
*RC Inc.	9/95	3,742	$ 67,181	1.5	$ 222,600
WW Grainger	10/98	4,257	$221,435	1.2	$ 311,293
Circuit City Stores	9/98	10,561	$304,062	1.2	$ 355,166
					$4,000,000

Kitty's Portfolio

Description	Acquired	Shares	Adjusted Basis	Beta	Current FMV
Tenet Health Care	1/92	2,542	$ 30,504	0.6	$ 50,209
Bay Bank Inc.	2/96	1,500	$120,000	0.5	$167,250
Microsoft	9/95	589	$ 53,010	0.7	$ 66,189
Zenith	10/97	22,190	$177,520	0.8	$216,352
					$500,000

*The RC Inc. stock is Section 1244 Small Business Stock.

QUESTIONS

1.   List the Remingtons' financial strengths and weaknesses.

    a.   Strengths:

    b.   Weaknesses:

2.   After reading the case, what additional information would you request from the Remingtons to complete your data-gathering phase?

3.   Assume that Wallace sells the K-Mart stock to Vicki for the current fair market value.   What are Wallace's tax consequences from this transaction?

4.   Assume that Wallace sells the K-Mart stock to Vicki for the fair market value as of January 1, 1999, and Vicki resells the K-Mart stock at $16.50 per share on December 15, 1999. What is the tax consequence to Vicki?

5.   If Wallace sells all of his RC Inc. stock this year (1999) at the current fair market value, what will be the tax treatment?

6.   Assume that on August 15, 1999, Wallace makes the following transactions in his stock portfolio. Assume that these are the Remingtons' only stock transactions for the year:

Sale Date	Stock	# of Shares	Sale Price Net Commissions
8/15/99	Sears	16,325	$840,000
8/15/99	WW Grainger	4,257	$320,000
8/15/99	Circuit City	10,561	$190,000

What are the tax consequences of these transactions?

7.   Assume that Wallace is now (January 1, 1999) contemplating donating $2,000,000 as a taxable gift to his grandson, Greg, in an irrevocable trust. Wallace wants to know how much he will pay out in total for such a gift, including the gift itself and any related taxes. Wallace has made no previous gifts to any grandchild. Wallace's total previous taxable gifts have amounted to $1,200,000. (Previous gift tax paid $235,000.) What is the projection of his total cash outflow from the above transaction?

8.   Wallace and Kitty want you to evaluate their insurance situation.

9.   Assuming that Wallace begins his single premium deferred annuity on the start date of January 1, 2000, what will be his tax consequences from the annuity payments received in 2000?

10.   In 2000 when Wallace returns from traveling and begins his consulting career, he expects to have taxable earned income of $100,000 per year. Describe the impact of his consulting activities.

11.   Using the Capital Asset Pricing Model, determine the expected return for Kitty's portfolio, assuming the market has a return that is 20% better than expected.

12.   If Wallace were to refinance his primary residence at current mortgage rates for 15 years, how much would his monthly payment decline?

13.   In 2000, Wallace will begin his consulting. Discuss his ability to defer taxes utilizing a qualified retirement plan.

14.   Which of the following transfers will not result in a taxable gift to Wallace in 1999, assuming he makes no other gifts?

      a.   Wallace pays each grandchild's private school tuition = $6,000 each.

      b.   Wallace pays City Hospital for the hospital bill of a friend = $12,000.

      c.   Wallace pays a distant cousin's law school tuition = $16,000.

      d.   Wallace pays the tuition for Wallace Jr. to Private University = $30,000.

15.   With regard to the installment sale portion of Wallace's interest in Remington Securities to Bob Newhart, how much, if any, of the down payment is taxable to Wallace in 1999, and what is the character of the down payment?

16.   Calculate the total monthly installment payments that will be made to Wallace by Newhart during 1999 (round to the nearest dollar).

17.   In 1999, how much will Wallace have to claim as ordinary income from the installment sale of Remington Securities?

18.   What is the impact of the survivorship clause in Wallace's will?

19.   Wallace and Kitty are considering the purchase of a joint and survivor (second-to-die) life insurance policy for the purpose of wealth replacement for the assets that were transferred to the CRAT and to help to create estate liquidity. Discuss the most appropriate way to own the joint and survivor life insurance to assure that the proceeds are not included in their estate.

20.   Assuming Wallace dies January 1, 2000 and Kitty survives him by six months, what is true regarding the installment sale to Bob Newhart?

21.   Wallace has paid his general liability insurance premiums for Remington Securities for two years in advance (January 1, 1999 - December 31, 2000). The premium for the two years was $144,000. At the time of his sale of the firm to Newhart and Pam, there will be a prepaid insurance amount. Wallace plans to assign the insurance policy to the new partnership of Pam and Newhart and thereby wants them to pay him for the remaining prepaid insurance premiums. Discuss the validity and effectiveness of the assignment of the policy.

22.   What is the likelihood that Wallace's 401(k) will yield a return that is below the Remingtons' required rate of return?

23.   Discuss the Remingtons' estate planning deficiencies.

24.   What estate planning recommendations would you make to the Remingtons?

25.   Explain the benefits of the GRAT established by Wallace.

26.   Calculate the gift tax that was saved using the GRAT over a straight outright gift. Do not include annual exclusions.

27.   What are the drawbacks in establishing a GRAT?

28.   What are the advantages of using a charitable remainder trust (CRT)?

29.   What investment planning recommendations would you make to the Remingtons?

30.   Calculate Wallace's Federal estate tax liability if he died today.

        Assumptions: Section 7520 rate = 8%

                        Life expectancy of Wallace = 17 years

THIS PAGE IS INTENTIONALLY LEFT BLANK.

AMY
DITKA

CASE SCENARIO AND QUESTIONS

AMY DITKA

Table of Contents

AMY DITKA

Case Scenario and Questions

Today is January 1, 1999. Amy Ditka has come to you, a financial planner, for help in developing a plan to accomplish her financial goals. From your initial meeting together, you have gathered the following information:

PERSONAL BACKGROUND AND INFORMATION

Amy Ditka (Age 69)

Amy is a retired homemaker. She is a recent widow. Amy's 70th birthday will be April 1, 1999.

Tim Ditka (deceased)

Amy was married to Tim Ditka, who died November 1, 1998, at the age of 69, after a brief battle with cancer. His date of birth was June 1, 1929.

Tim's estate is in probate. Tim was employed 45 years as a supervisor at ABC Co., Inc. (ABC) before retiring at age 65.

The Ditkas

They were married 50 years. Amy's health is fair.

The Ditkas' Children

Amy has two children from her marriage to Tim: George (Age 50) and Vince (Age 49). George and Vince are each married, healthy, employed, and self-sufficient.

The Ditkas' Grandchildren

George and his wife, Kathy, have one daughter, Sarah (Age 18). Sarah is currently a senior in high school and will be a freshman at Private University in the fall. The cost of tuition for Private University is currently $12,000. Amy would like to pay the university for Sarah's tuition for this year. As a graduation present, Amy is paying for Sarah's trip to Europe this summer. The cost of this trip is $3,000.

Vince and his wife, Laena, have one son, Kirby (Age 17). Kirby is a junior in high school. Kirby is in need of orthodontic work that will cost $6,000. Amy would like to pay the orthodontist for Kirby's orthodontic work. Amy is also considering gifting stock worth $9,000 to Kirby because she wishes to treat each grandchild equally.

PERSONAL AND FINANCIAL OBJECTIVES

- Amy wants to have sufficient income ($30,000 per year in today's dollars including any Social Security benefits).
- Amy will consider acquiring a smaller residence.
- Amy wants to explore long-term nursing care alternatives (annual cost in today's dollars $40,000).
- Amy wants to donate to the American Cancer Society.
- Amy wants to provide for her children and grandchildren.
- Amy wants to pay Sarah's tuition ($12,000).
- Amy wants to gift stock to Kirby ($9,000).
- Amy wants to pay for Kirby's orthodontic work ($6,000).
- Amy wants to send Sarah to Europe ($3,000).

ECONOMIC INFORMATION

- Inflation is expected to be 4% annually.
- There is no state income tax.
- A slow growth economy is expected, and stocks are expected to grow at 9.5%.

Bank lending rates are as follows:
- 15-year mortgages 7.5%.
- 30-year mortgages 8.0%.
- Secured personal loan 10.0%.

Life Expectancies from IRS (Table V)

Age	Life Expectancy Factor
69	16.8
70	16.0
71	15.3

INSURANCE INFORMATION

Life Insurance

Irrevocable Life Insurance Trust (ILIT)

Tim created an ILIT 10 years ago. The only asset in the trust is a permanent life policy with a face value of $200,000. The income beneficiary of the ILIT is Amy. She is also the trustee and has a general power of appointment over the trust assets. The remainder beneficiaries are the grandchildren.

Health Insurance

Tim and Amy were both covered under Medicare Part A.

INVESTMENT INFORMATION

Amy's investment risk tolerance is low.

INCOME TAX INFORMATION

The Ditkas filed as married filing jointly for 1997. Amy and Tim have always lived in a community property state.

RETIREMENT INFORMATION

Tim had a pension with ABC with Amy designated as the beneficiary. The pension currently has a lump sum death benefit of $150,000. As the beneficiary, Amy can choose to receive a life annuity or a lump sum payment from the pension.

Amy currently has an IRA with Tim as the named beneficiary. Amy is the named beneficiary on Tim's IRA.

Both Tim and Amy began receiving Social Security benefits on their respective 65th birthdays. Tim's benefit for 1999 would have been $1,200 per month, and Amy's benefit for 1999 was estimated to be $600 per month.

GIFTS, ESTATES, TRUSTS, AND WILL INFORMATION

Tim's will left all probate assets to Amy. The grandchildren are named as contingent beneficiaries (equally).

Amy does not have a will.

STATEMENT OF FINANCIAL POSITION

Tim (deceased) and Amy Ditka
Balance Sheet
As of January 1, 1999

ASSETS[1]			LIABILITIES & NET WORTH		
Cash and Equivalents			**Liabilities[2]**		
CP	Cash	$ 25,000	Credit Cards[5]	$	20,000
CP	Savings Account	20,000			
	Total Cash and Equivalents	$ 45,000			
	Invested Assets				
H	Stocks	$ 20,000	*Total Liabilities*	$	20,000
W	IRA	40,000			
H	IRA	50,000			
CP	Pension	150,000	**Net Worth**	$	80,000
	Total Invested Assets	$ 260,000			
	Personal Use Assets				
CP	Primary Residence[3]	$ 400,000			
W	Vacation Home[4]	200,000			
CP	Auto	18,000			
CP	Furniture & Personal Property	77,000			
	Total Use Of Assets	$ 695,000			
			Total Liabilities &		
	Total Assets	$1,000,000	**Net Worth**	$1,000,000	

Notes to Financial Statements:
1 Assets are stated at fair market value.
2 Liabilities are stated at principal only as of January 1, 1999 before January payments. All liabilities are community property.
3 The primary residence was originally purchased for $110,000. There have been no additions or upgrades.
4 The vacation home was inherited by Amy from her mother. Adjusted taxable basis is $125,000.
5 Interest rate 18.3%.

Other Notes to Financial Statements:
The $200,000 ILIT is the separate property of Tim; the income beneficiary is Amy. Remainder beneficiaries are the grandchildren. Amy has general power of appointment over trust assets. Trustee has power to invade for HEMS (health, education, maintenance, or support) for the grandchildren. The ILIT is not listed on the Balance Sheet.

INFORMATION REGARDING ASSETS AND LIABILITIES

Primary Residence

- Purchased April 1, 1965.
- Market value $400,000 as of November 1, 1998 and June 1, 1999.
- Original purchase price $110,000.

Vacation Home

- Owned by Amy (fee simple).
- Inherited from her mother. (The fair market value at the date of transfer to Amy was $125,000 in July 1984.)
- The current fair market value is $200,000.
- The vacation home is located in a non-community property state. All payments for repairs and maintenance have been made using community property assets.

QUESTIONS

1.   List Amy's financial strengths and weaknesses.

   a.   Strengths:

   b.   Weaknesses:

2.   After reading the case, what additional information would you request from Amy to complete your data-gathering phase?

3.   Calculate the following financial ratios for Amy.

$$\frac{\text{Net Worth}}{\text{Total Assets}} \quad =$$

$$\frac{\text{Total Debt}}{\text{Total Assets}} \quad =$$

$$\frac{\text{Investment Assets}}{\text{Total Assets}} \quad =$$

4.   Comment on any of the above ratios that you think are important.

5.   What are Amy's options with regard to Tim's IRA?

6.   Amy plans to delay the initial distribution from her IRA account until April 1, 2000. How much will she have to distribute, at a minimum, in the year 2000, assuming she calculates the distribution over a single life expectancy without recalculation and the IRA has the following account balances:

	1998 (year-end)	1999 (year-end)	2000 (year-end)
IRA Account Balance	$40,000	$50,000	$60,000

7.   Calculate Amy's probate estate as of today assuming the pension plan is heritable from Amy to her heirs.

8.   Calculate Amy's gross estate as of today assuming the pension plan is heritable from Amy to her heirs.

9.   Which post-mortem devices should Amy seriously consider with regards
        to Tim's estate?

10.   Amy is considering selling her personal residence.   What is Amy's
        adjusted taxable basis for the personal residence?

11.   What is the titling nature of the vacation home property at Tim's death?

12.   Amy is considering establishing a charitable trust for the American
       Cancer Society but wants the grandchildren to receive income from the
       property for a 20-year period. Which devices would be appropriate to
       meet Amy's objective?

13.   If Amy exercised her right to take a lump sum cash distribution from
       Tim's pension plan, how much money will she actually receive from the
       plan?

14.   Which Social Security benefits does Amy currently qualify for?

15.   What happens to Amy's IRA upon her death, assuming she makes no changes to the account?

16.   Assuming that Amy has taken a lump sum distribution from Tim's pension plan, what combination of investments is appropriate for Amy?

17.   How could Amy benefit each grandchild equally without incurring any transfer taxes or utilizing her unified credit equivalency?

18.   What is Amy's Federal income tax filing status for the years 1998, 1999, 2000, and 2001?

19.   How much will Amy's monthly Social Security benefit be in 1999?

20.   On November 1, 1999, Amy decides to sell her personal residence for the FMV as of January 1, 1999. What will be her tax consequences?

21. Amy is very concerned about her long-term health and is considering buying a Medicare Part B policy. Which benefits are covered under Medicare Part B?

22. Amy has purchased a Medicare Part B policy but is still concerned about the deductibles and co-pay requirements. She is considering either purchasing a Medigap policy or joining a Medicare HMO. What are the advantage(s) of an HMO over a Medigap policy in Amy's situation?

23. Amy is worried that she will need long-term custodial care because while her mother lived at home until age 95 she needed assistance in bathing, dressing, and toileting once she became 75 years old. Amy is worried that there will be no family member around to care for her. What insurance would provide Amy with such continued assistance in her home?

24.   At her death, Amy wants to maximize her benefit to the American Cancer Society and at the same time maximize benefits to her children and grandchildren. Which assets would be best left to the American Cancer Society?

WILLIAM AND MARILYN MATHEWS

CASE SCENARIO AND QUESTIONS

WILLIAM AND MARILYN MATHEWS

Table of Contents

The following case scenario appeared on CFP Board Comprehensive CFP® Certification Examinations. The case has been approved for publication by the CFP Board of Examiners. If you have a question about the technical content of the case, please address your question to the Board of Examiners by <u>writing</u> to them at the CFP Board address:

1700 Broadway, Suite 2100
Denver, CO 80290-2101

CFP® and Certified Financial Planner® are Federally registered service marks of the Certified Financial Planner Board of Standards, Inc. (CFP Board).

WILLIAM AND MARILYN MATHEWS

Case Scenario and Questions

Your clients, Bill and Marilyn Mathews, have asked you to help them with a number of issues facing them as Bill prepares to sell his business and formally retire. Marilyn will also retire, having worked as the company bookkeeper for twenty years. Negotiations for the sale of Bill's business, Calculator City, are almost concluded, pending resolution of a number of questions Bill raised regarding installment payments for the business as well as a request from the proposed owner that Bill continue to provide consulting services.

PERSONAL BACKGROUND AND INFORMATION

	Age	Health	Occupation
William Mathews	65	Excellent	Business Owner
Marilyn Mathews	63	"	Bookkeeper
John Mathews (son)	32	"	Engineer
James Mathews (son)	30	"	CPA
Grandchildren	3, 4, 5, and 7	"	

Neither son has any intention of becoming involved in the business. The Mathews file a joint tax return. Client and spouse have simple wills leaving all to each other.

ECONOMIC INFORMATION

The current economic environment exhibits low real short-term rates, high real long-term rates, little economic growth, and high unemployment.

PERSONAL AND FINANCIAL OBJECTIVES

1.   Maintain current lifestyle, including frequent travel.

2.   Revise estate plan to minimize taxes, take advantage of opportunities in various elections available in the Internal Revenue Code, and maximize amounts passing to children and grandchildren.

3.   Review investment portfolio and make changes as necessary to reflect different priorities and risk tolerance levels during retirement. Initial indications are that the clients are willing to take normal investment risks, desirous of adequate current income, reasonable safety of principal, inflation protection, tax advantage, and some modest long-term appreciation, in that order of priority.

4.   Review and revise total risk management and insurance situation as necessary to provide adequate protection, and eliminate gaps and overlaps.

5.   Determine the most advantageous method of taking distributions from the 401(k) accounts.

STATEMENT OF FINANCIAL POSITION

William and Marilyn Mathews
As of December 31, 1992

ASSETS		LIABILITIES AND NET WORTH	
Invested Assets			
Cash/Cash Equivalents	$ 8,000	Auto Loan	$ 6,000
Marketable Securities[1]	1,580,000	Mortgage [2]	12,000
Business Interest [3]	1,500,000	Mortgage[4]	74,000
Life Ins. Cash Value[5]	60,000		$ 92,000
Annuity	120,000		
	$3,268,000		
Use Assets			
Primary Residence	$ 188,000		
Summer Home	126,000		
Personal Property	60,000		
Automobiles	26,000	Net Worth	$3,951,000
	$ 400,000		
Retirement Plan Assets[6]			
IRA (H)	$ 27,000		
IRA (W)	28,000		
401(k) (H)	280,000		
401(k) (W)	40,000		
	$ 375,000		
		Total Liabilities	
Total Assets	**$4,043,000**	**and Net Worth**	**$4,043,000**

---

1 See separate Investment Portfolio Supplement.

2 Principal residence; originally, 30 years @ 7%.

3 Business is to be sold for $1.5 million. Purchase price was $700,000 in 1982. Terms of sale include $300,000 down payment on July 1, 1993, with the balance to be paid over 120 months starting August 1, 1993, at 10% interest.

4 Summer home; originally, 15 years @ 9%.

5 Face Amount: $200,000; Bill is insured, Marilyn is beneficiary.

6 Spouse is beneficiary for IRA and 401(k). The IRAs are invested in a common stock growth mutual fund. The 401(k) plans are invested in three year Treasury notes.

STATEMENT OF CASH FLOWS

William and Marilyn Mathews
1/1/93 through 12/31/93 (Projected - Monthly)

(Incomplete)

Cash Inflows

Social Security (H)	$ 820
Social Security (W)	410
Installment Payments (120 pmts @ 10%)	?
Interest Income (tax-exempt)	600
Dividend Income	540
Interest Income (taxable)	?
Other Investment Income	?

Outflows

Savings and Investment	?
Mortgage (residence: PITI)	600
Mortgage (summer home: PITI)	1,100
Food	300
Utilities	400
Transportation (gas, oil, maintenance)	200
Car Payment	600
Clothing	250
Entertainment	450
Travel	1,680
Family Gifts	1,666
Charitable Gifts	500
Life Insurance	300
Hospitalization (Medigap/Medicare)	100
Automobile Insurance	150
Miscellaneous	?
Federal Income Tax	5,800
State Income Tax	900
Other	?

INSURANCE AND ANNUITY INFORMATION

Life Insurance

Person Insured/Owner	Bill
Type of Policy	Whole Life
Face Amount	$200,000
Dividend Option	Paid Up Additions
Issue Date	2/13/77
Beneficiary	Marilyn
Current Cash Value	$60,000
Premium	$300 per month

Person Insured/Owner	Bill
Type of Policy	Single Premium Deferred Annuity
Fixed or Variable	Fixed
Current Value	$120,000
Current Interest Rate	6.5%
Issue Date	1/1/81
Purchase Price	$40,000

Homeowners Insurance

Homeowners Policy	
Type	HO-3
Amount on Dwelling	$175,000
Personal Property Coverage	$ 87,500
Personal Liability	$100,000

Automobile Insurance

Type	Personal Auto Policy
Bodily Injury/Property Damage	$300,000 Combined Single Limit
Collision	$250 Deductible
Comprehensive	Full, with $100 Deductible
Uninsured Motorist	$300,000 Single Limit

INVESTMENT INFORMATION

These securities were accumulated over a period of years and are essentially unmanaged.

Common Stocks	Fair Market Value
AT & T	$ 30,000
Bell South	10,000
Bell Atlantic	9,000
Ameritech	8,500
NYNEX	7,000
Pacific Telesis	8,000
Southwestern Bell	8,000
U.S. West	7,000
Canon	22,000
Comerica Bank	29,000
Danko	7,000
de Beers	8,000
du Pont	29,000
Disney	12,000
Dow Chemical	9,000
Detroit Edison	24,000
General Motors	8,000
GM E	10,500
D&T, Inc.*	25,000
Common stock mutual fund (IRAs)	55,000

Municipal Bonds	
Franklin Intermediate Tax Exempt Fund	100,000

Annuities & Insurance	
Cash value life insurance	60,000
Single Premium Deferred Annuity	120,000

Bonds	
Treasury notes (401(k))	20,000
U.S. EE Savings Bonds	75,000

Cash and Equivalents	
Cash	8,000
Cash equivalents, incl. Money Markets	134,000
Treasury Securities (T-Bills)	1,000,000
TOTAL	**$2,143,000**

*Small Business Corporation (1244 stock) solely owned by Bill and originally purchased for $76,000 on 1/1/87.

QUESTIONS

Questions 1- 19 appeared on CFP Board Comprehensive CFP® Certification Examinations. The questions have been approved for publication by the CFP Board of Examiners. If you have a question about the technical content of the case, please address your question to the Board of Examiners by <u>writing</u> to them at the CFP Board address:

1700 Broadway, Suite 2100
Denver, CO 80290-2101

CFP® and Certified Financial Planner® are Federally registered service marks of the Certified Financial Planner Board of Standards, Inc. (CFP Board).

The [   ] areas have been modified from the original released case for the sole purpose of accommodating a non-multiple choice format. The intent of the question has not been altered.

1.   [Discuss the tax treatment of the down payment made to Bill for the sale of his business.]

2.   How much will Bill receive from the monthly installment payments during 1993 (rounded to the nearest dollar)?

3. [What is the approximate amount of interest income from the installment sale for the year ending December 31, 1993?]

4. How will Bill's receipt of installment payments for the sale of his business affect his Social Security benefits?

5. Bill and Marilyn both have account balances in the 401(k) Plan, and they want to determine what options they can pursue. [Discuss the options available for Bill and Marilyn.]

6.   The Mathews family is considering the purchase of a survivorship life insurance policy, payable on the second death of either Bill or Marilyn, for the primary purpose of providing liquidity for the payment of the Federal estate tax.   The ownership and beneficiary arrangements are being studied for the best overall result. [Discuss which options for ownership and beneficiary arrangements are viable.]

7.   If Bill decides to make a partial withdrawal from his Single Premium Deferred Annuity, what income tax result will ensue?

8.   Bill is contemplating selling his D&T, Inc. stock for the fair market value. [Assuming he sold D&T on December 31, 1992, discuss the tax impact.]

9.   [In view of the combined estate values for Bill and Marilyn, discuss the most appropriate estate planning techniques.]

10.   The Mathews currently own a number of tax-advantaged financial instruments. [Discuss the various instruments available.]

11.   If Bill and Marilyn wish to limit the growth of their combined estate, which techniques may be advisable?

12. Assume that Bill wants to take advantage of the $1,000,000 Generation Skipping Transfer Tax exemption, by giving his grandson this amount now. What is the amount of the gift tax, given that there have been no prior taxable gifts?

13. Assume Bill provides consulting services for the new owner and is properly classified as an independent contractor. [Discuss Bill's ability to shelter current taxable income.]

14. In reviewing Bill and Marilyn's cash-flow projections as well as the investment portfolio supplement, you question the appropriateness of some of the holdings. What combination of portfolio weaknesses best summarizes a valid critique of their investments?

15. Assuming that Bill reaches an agreement with the new owner as to the installment payments for the business interest, what are the estate tax ramifications if Bill dies at the end of the third year of the ten-year payout schedule?

16. [What are the inadequacies in their estate planning?]

Regarding questions 17 and 18 and given the current economic conditions, you recommend allocating the Mathews' investment funds into three asset categories: equity, debt, and cash.

17.   [What action(s) would you recommend regarding asset allocation in order to meet the Mathews' goals?]

18.   [Explain what the Mathews should do in order to meet their goals.]

19.   You are considering liquidating the individual equity holdings and moving this amount into equity mutual funds. The following alternative allocations have been proposed:

Choice A		Choice B	
Market index fund	40%	Growth fund	33%
Growth fund	20%	International equity fund	33%
Value-oriented fund	20%	Value-oriented fund	34%
International equity fund	20%		
Choice C		**Choice D**	
Market index fund	30%	Small company fund	25%
Gold stock fund	50%	Aggressive growth fund	45%
Equity-income fund	20%	Growth fund	30%

The following questions have been added by Michael A. Dalton and are not from the CFP Board of Standards.

20.   List the Mathews' financial strengths and weaknesses.

     a.   Strengths:

     b.   Weaknesses:

21.   After reading the case, what additional information would you request from the Mathews to complete your data-gathering phase?

22.   Identify the best choices of investments for this current economic environment. Explain your choices.

23.   Assume that the Mathews had a substantial charitable intent but were concerned with the loss of wealth to their children. What estate and insurance planning device could they use to provide estate liquidity and wealth replacement for any charitable contributions as well as provide them with a current income tax deduction and retirement income?

24.   Evaluate the Mathews' current investment portfolio and recommend any changes.

25.   Evaluate the Mathews' current insurance situation.

26.   What would be some alternatives to the installment sale, presuming one or more of the children had an interest in the business and William wanted to remove the value of the business from his estate were he to die?

27.   What if the DAT stock (Section 1244 stock) was sold for a gain?

28.   Assume that all assets are community property and that William dies with his current will. Determine the value of William's gross estate. Assume that funeral and administrative expenses total $100,000.

29.   Assume that all assets are community property and that William dies with his current will. Determine the estate tax liability for William's estate. Assume that funeral and administrative expenses total $100,000.

30.   Assume that all assets are community property and that William dies with his current will and that Marilyn dies shortly thereafter. Determine the value of Marilyn's gross estate. Assume that funeral and administrative expenses total $100,000 for both.

31.   Assume that all assets are community property and that William dies with his current will and that Marilyn dies shortly thereafter. Determine the estate tax liability for Marilyn's estate. Assume that funeral and administrative expenses total $100,000 for both.

32.   Based upon Question 31, how much could have been saved in estate tax liability assuming that you arranged the estate any way you wished? Furthermore, the assets would remain at exactly the same value, and the Mathews die 3½ years from now.

33.   After reviewing the Mathews' current income tax situation, what would you recommend they do in contemplation of the installment sale?

APPENDIX

TABLE OF EXHIBITS

EXHIBIT 1: FUNDAMENTALS - HOUSING COSTS AND DEBT REPAYMENT

Indicators of Financial Strengths and Weaknesses

As a % of Gross Income

| | Weaknesses | | Neutral | Strengths | |
	Extreme	Moderate		Moderate	Extreme
	≥	≥	≤	≤	≤
Housing Costs	40%	35%	30%	28%	20%
Housing Costs Plus Other Debt Repayments	48%	43%	38%	36%	28%

- Housing costs include principal payments, interest, taxes, insurance, and any association dues or costs.

- The total of all housing costs as a % of monthly gross income generally must be ≤ 28% to qualify for a mortgage.

- Other debt repayments include credit card payments, automobile loan payments, student loan payments, and the like.

- The combination of housing costs and other monthly debt repayments generally must be ≤ 36% of monthly gross income to qualify for a home mortgage.

EXHIBIT 2: INSURANCE - SUMMARY OF VARIOUS COMPANY RATINGS

Rank	A. M. Best	Best's Description	D & P	Moody's	S&P	Weiss	Weiss's Description
1	A++	Superior	AAA	Aaa	AAA	A+	Excellent
2	A+	Superior	AA+	Aa1	AA+	A	Excellent
3	A	Excellent	AA	Aa2	AA	A-	Excellent
4	A-	Excellent	AA-	Aa3	AA-	B+	Good
5	B++	Very Good	A+	A1	A+	B	Good
6	B+	Very Good	A	A2	A	B-	Good
7	B	Good	A-	A3	A-	C+	Fair
8	B-	Good	BBB+	Baa1	BBB+	C	Fair
9	C++	Fair	BBB	Baa2	BBB	C-	Fair
10	C+	Fair	BBB-	Baa3	BBB-	D+	Weak
11	C	Marginal	BB+	Ba1	BB+	D	Weak
12	C-	Marginal	BB	Ba2	BB	D-	Weak
13	D	Below Min. Standards	BB-	Ba3	BB-	E+	Very Weak
14	E	Under State Supervision	B+	B1	B+	E	Very Weak
15	F	In Liquidation	B	B2	B	E-	Very Weak
16						F	Under Supervision

Rating Companies

a. A. M. Best Company - Ratings are based on public information and interviews with management.

b. Duff & Phelps Credit Rating Company - Uses public information and management interviews. Public information alone may be used to assign ratings.

c. Moody's Investors Service - May assign ratings based on public information alone.

d. Standard & Poor's Corporation - Rates companies only upon request.

e. Weiss Research - Ratings are based on public information and proprietary methods of evaluation and are available only on a company-by-company basis.

EXHIBIT 3: INSURANCE - LIFE INSURANCE POLICY REPLACEMENT - THE BASICS

The decision to replace one policy with another should be made cautiously. The methodology for such a decision includes fact gathering, calculations, and benchmark comparisons.

The Belth price of protection model formula:

$$CPT = \frac{(P + CV_0)(1 + i) - (CV_1 + D)}{(DB - CV_1)(0.001)}$$

Where:

CPT	=	cost per thousand.
P	=	annual premium.
CV_0	=	cash value at beginning of year.
i	=	net after tax earning rate.
CV_1	=	cash value at year-end.
D	=	current dividend.
DB	=	death benefit.

Compare to benchmark table:

- If cost < benchmark price, then retain policy.
- If cost > benchmark but < 2 x benchmark, then retain policy.
- If cost > 2 x benchmark consider replacement.

Table (Joseph M. Belth, author)

Benchmark Price	Price of Insurance per $1,000
Age < 30	1.50
30-34	2.00
35-39	3.00
40-44	4.00
45-49	6.50
50-54	10.00
55-59	15.00
60-64	25.00
65-69	35.00
70-74	50.00
75-79	80.00
80-84	125.00

EXHIBIT 4: INSURANCE - SUMMARY OF HOMEOWNER'S INSURANCE POLICIES

	HO1 (Basic Form)	HO2 (Broad Form)	HO3 (Special Form)	HO8 (For Older Homes)	HO4 (Renter's Contents Broad Form)	HO6 (For Condominium Owners)
Perils covered (descriptions are given below)	Perils 1 - 12	Perils 1 - 18	All perils except those specifically excluded from buildings; perils 1-18 on personal property.	Perils 1 - 12	Perils 1 - 18	Perils 1 - 18
Property coverages/limits						
House and any other attached buildings	Amount based on replacement cost, minimum $15,000	Amount based on replacement cost, minimum $15,000	Amount based on replacement cost, minimum $20,000	Amount based on actual cash value of the home, minimum $15,000	Not Applicable	$1,000 on owner's additions and alterations to the unit
Detached buildings	10% of insurance on the home	10 % of insurance on the home	10% of insurance on the home	10% of insurance on the home	Not covered	Included in coverage of Part A
Trees, shrubs, plants, etc.	5% of insurance on the home, $500 maximum per item	5% of insurance on the home, $500 maximum per item	5% of insurance on the home, $500 maximum per item	5% of insurance on the home, $500 maximum per item	10% of personal property insurance, $500 maximum per item	10% of personal property insurance, $500 maximum per item
Personal Property	50% of insurance on the home	50% of insurance on the home	50% of insurance on the home	50% of insurance on the home	Chosen by the tenant to reflect the value of the items, minimum $6,000	Chosen by home owner to reflect the value of the items, minimum $6,000
Loss of use and/or add'l living expense	10% of insurance on the home	20% of insurance on the home	20% of insurance on the home	10% of insurance on the home	20% of personal property insurance	40% of personal property insurance
Credit card, forgery, counterfeit money	$500	$500	$500	$500	$500	$500
Liability coverages/limits						
Comprehensive personal liability	$25,000 - $100,000	$25,000 - $100,000	$25,000 - $100,000	$25,000 - $100,000	$25,000 - $100,000	$25,000 - $100,000
Damage to property of others	$250 - $500	$250 - $500	$250 - $500	$250 - $500	$250 - $500	$250 - $500
Medical payments	$500 - $1,000	$500 - $1,000	$500 - $1,000	$500 - $1,000	$500 - $1,000	$500 - $1,000
Special limits of liability*	Special limits apply on a per-occurrence basis (e.g., per fire or theft): money, coins, bank notes, precious metals (gold, silver, etc.), securities, deeds, stocks, bonds, tickets, stamps; watercraft and trailers, including furnishings, equipment, and outboard motors; trailers other than for watercraft; jewelry, watches, furs; silverware, goldware, etc.; guns.					

EXHIBIT 5: INSURANCE - LIST OF COVERED PERILS

BASIC NAMED PERILS		
1. Fire	5. Riot or civil commotion	9. Vandalism or malicious mischief
2. Lightning	6. Aircraft	10. Explosion
3. Windstorm	7. Vehicles	11. Theft
4. Hail	8. Smoke	12. Volcanic eruption

BROAD NAMED PERILS
Basic Named Perils 1 - 12
13. Falling objects
14. Weight of ice, snow, sleet
15. Accidental discharge or overflow of water or stream
16. Sudden and accidental tearing apart, cracking, burning, or bulging of a steam, hot water, air conditioning, or automatic fire protective sprinkler system, or from within a household appliance
17. Freezing of a plumbing, heating, air conditioning, or automatic fire sprinkler system, or of a household appliance
18. Sudden and accidental damage from artificially generated electrical current

	HO1*	HO2	HO3	HO4	HO6	HO8
Coverage A - Dwelling	Basic	Broad	Open Peril	N/A	Broad	Basic
Coverage B - Other Structures	Basic	Broad	Open Peril	N/A	N/A	Basic
Coverage C - Personal Property	Basic	Broad	Broad	Broad	Broad	Basic
Coverage D - Loss of Use	Basic	Broad	Open Peril/ Broad	Broad	Broad	Basic

*HO1 is no longer commonly sold.

EXHIBIT 6: INSURANCE - EIGHT GENERAL EXCLUSIONS FOR HOMEOWNERS

• Ordinance or Law	• Neglect
• Earth Movement	• War
• Water Damage	• Nuclear Hazard
• Power Failure	• Intentional Loss

EXHIBIT 7: INVESTMENTS - TOTAL RISK

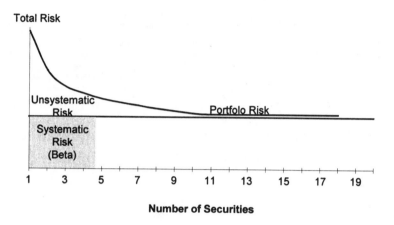

Number of Securities

EXHIBIT 8: INVESTMENTS - SYSTEMATIC AND UNSYSTEMATIC RISKS

Systematic Risks	Unsystematic Risks
Market Risk	Business Risk
Interest Rate Risk	Financial Risk
Purchasing Power Risk	Default Risk
Foreign Currency Risk	Regulation Risk
Reinvestment Rate Risk	

EXHIBIT 9: INVESTMENTS - THE CALL OPTION

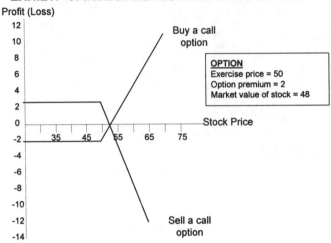

The exhibit above depicts the profit (loss) for both a buyer and a seller of a call option. Notice that the buyer has unlimited profit potential while the seller has unlimited loss potential. Likewise, the buyer's loss and the seller's gain are limited to the premium paid.

EXHIBIT 10: INVESTMENTS - THE PUT OPTION

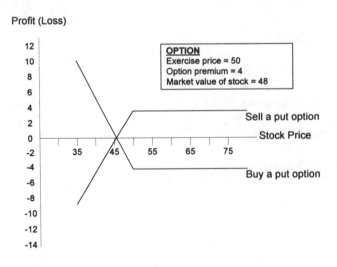

The exhibit above depicts the profit (loss) for both a buyer and a seller of a put option. Notice that the buyer has a large profit potential while the seller has a large loss potential. Likewise, the buyer's loss and the seller's gain are limited to the premium paid.

EXHIBIT 11: INVESTMENTS - AREA UNDER THE CURVE

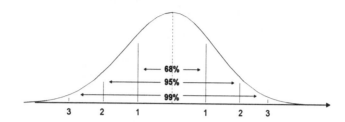

- The curve represents 100% of possible outcomes. These outcomes tend to cluster around the mean; however, some occurrences will fall away from the mean (i.e., in the tails of the bell shaped curve).

- Approximately 68% of outcomes will fall within one standard deviation (both above and below) of the mean.

- **Note:** One standard deviation will be different for each individual security and may have a wide range.

- Approximately 95% of outcomes will fall within two standard deviations (both above and below) of the mean.

- Approximately 99% of outcomes will fall within three standard deviations (both above and below) of the mean.

- This information about the normal curve allows investors to determine the probability of specific outcomes.

EXHIBIT 12: INVESTMENTS - STANDARD DEVIATION OF TWO SECURITIES

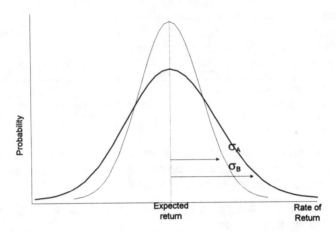

The exhibit above illustrates that two securities can have the same expected return with different levels of risk. Security B is more risky than Security A because its standard deviation is greater.

EXHIBIT 13: INVESTMENTS - EXPLANATION OF STANDARD DEVIATION AND EXPECTED RETURN

Standard deviation is calculated by taking the square root of the sum of the squared differences between the average return, which will remain constant, and the individual observations (or returns) divided by the number of observations minus one. This calculation can be done in five steps:

1. For each observation, take the difference between the average return and the individual observations.

2. Square each difference.

3. Sum the squared differences.

4. Divide this sum by one less than the number of observations (if there is 10 observations, divide by 9).

5. Take the square root of this division.

Note 1: Certain requirements must be met to use this technique with accuracy.

Note 2: The standard deviation equals the square root of the variance. Thus, step iv. is equal to the variance, and step v. is equal to the standard deviation.

Expected return is calculated by summing the product of the probability of an occurrence and the occurrence. For example, the following observations: 9, 11, 13 with the following probabilities: 0.25, 0.50, 0.25 will yield an expected return of 11. This is calculated as follows: (0.25 x 9) + (0.50 x 11) + (0.25 x 13) = 11.

Note: The standard deviation for a set of investment returns can be calculated very efficiently using a financial calculator, such as a HP 12C. Using the above information, the keystrokes would be:

	f	clx (clears registers)
	13.5	$\Sigma+$
	12.0	$\Sigma+$
	5.0	$\Sigma+$
	(2.0)	$\Sigma+$
	7.0	$\Sigma+$
	23.0	$\Sigma+$
	6.0	$\Sigma+$
	10.0	$\Sigma+$
	45.0	$\Sigma+$
	10.0	$\Sigma+$
	0.5	$\Sigma+$
	14.0	$\Sigma+$

To determine the mean: g   0

To determine the standard deviation: g   . (period)

The result will be the same as calculating the standard deviation by longhand.

EXHIBIT 14: INVESTMENTS - PERFORMANCE MEASUREMENTS

1.   **Single-Period Rate of Return.**
    a.   The single period return (also known as the holding period return) is the basic method to evaluate the speed at which an investment grows or declines.   The single period return is determined by dividing the change in wealth by the initial investment.
    b.   The formula for the single period rate of return is:

$$\frac{(SP - PP + CF)}{PP} \text{ , where:}$$

SP = The current sales price for the asset.
PP = The initial purchase price of the asset.
CF =   Any cash flows that occurred during the holding period, such as dividends, interest, or other income.

    c.   The holding period return (single period rate of return) refers to the overall percentage gain the investor has received. The holding period return is not often used as a measure of performance because it ignores the time value of money, and it does not address the time over which the investment has grown.

2.   **Arithmetic Average Return.**
    a.   The arithmetic average return, which is the same as a normal average or mean, is equal to the sum of the returns per interval divided by the number of observations.   For example, the average return for the following set of data would be approximately 12.41%.

1992	1993	1994	1995	1996	1997	1998	1999
12.1%	10.0%	11.3%	15.2%	9.1%	6.5%	18.3%	16.8%

    b.   The arithmetic average return is an approximation of the earnings rate for an investment over time.   However, large fluctuations in returns from year to year, especially negative returns, will have a tendency to cause the arithmetic return to be incorrect.

3.   **Geometric Average Return.**
   a.   Geometric average return is the average compounded return or the internal rate of return (annualized return). This return is calculated by subtracting 1 from the $1/n^{th}$ root of the product of each interval return plus 1. Therefore, the geometric average return for the data above is equal to $[(1 + 0.121) \times (1 + 0.100) \times (1 + 0.113) \times (1 + 0.152) \times (1 + 0.091) \times (1 + 0.065) \times (1 + 0.183) \times (1 + 0.168)]^{1/8} - 1$. Thus, the compound annual return is equal to 12.35%.

   b.   The reason the arithmetic and geometric average returns are different is that the arithmetic return does not take into consideration the compounding effect of the returns.

   c.   The geometric return is the same as the IRR or annual compound return.

4.   **Real Return (inflation adjusted).**

   a.   The loss of purchasing power is one of the risks that investors face in achieving their financial goals. Real returns reflect the excess earnings from an investment that are above the inflation rate. However, simply subtracting the rate of inflation from the investment rate of return will not yield the real return.

   b.   The real return can be calculated using the formula:

$$\left[\frac{(1 + \text{nominal return})}{(1 + \text{inflation rate})} - 1 \right] \times 100 \quad , \text{where:}$$

   Nominal rate = The absolute return (in the example above, it was 10%).

5.   **Total Return.**
   The total return for any investment can be thought of as the sum of the appreciation and the earnings from that investment. For stocks, this would be the appreciation in stock price plus dividends received. Similarly, the total return for bonds includes appreciation and interest payments. These two components are taken into consideration in the basic present value model discussed earlier.

6.   **Internal Rate of Return (IRR).**
   a.   The IRR is the earnings rate at which the present value of a series of cash flows will equal its cost. Recall the basic model or determining the present value of a series of cash flows.
   b.   The Basic Model:

$$P_0 = \frac{CF_1}{(1+k)^1} + \frac{CF_2}{(1+k)^2} + \cdots + \frac{CF_t}{(1+k)^t} \text{, where:}$$

   P_0 =   The value of the security today.
   CF_t =   The cash flow for period t.
   k   =   The discount rate or internal rate of return.
   t   =   The number of cash flows to be evaluated.

   c.   The underlying assumption of this equation is that the cash flows that occur during the life of the investment will be reinvested at the investment's internal rate of return. This is the same assumption found in computing the yield to maturity.

7.   **Time Weighted vs. Dollar Weighted.**
The internal rate of return is a dollar weighted return since it takes into consideration the different cash flows of the investor. A time-weighted return is determined without regard to the cash flows of the investor. It is a measure of the performance of an investment over a period of time, without regard to specific cash flows. It can be used to determine how well an investment has done over a period of time. For example, most returns reported on mutual funds are time-weighted returns.

8.   **Tax-Adjusted Returns.**
A tax-adjusted return is the realized return multiplied by (1 – tax rate). It is important to factor in taxes when comparing one investment alternative to another. For example, the after-tax yield on a municipal bond may be higher than for a corporate bond, even though the corporate bond carries a higher stated rate of return or has a higher yield to maturity.
The after tax return should reflect both Federal and local taxes.
Non taxable income.
   a.   Federal - The interest from municipal bonds is not taxable by the Federal government. In addition, unrealized appreciation is not taxable by the Federal government.
   b.   Municipalities - The interest from Treasury bills, bonds, and notes, as well as savings bonds, is not taxable by states and municipalities. Additionally, most municipalities do not tax interest from municipal bonds issued by its own government.

9.   **Risk Adjusted Returns.**
        It is important to compare or benchmark returns with some standard,
        such as the S&P 500 index. As mentioned above, it is also important to
        compare after-tax returns of different investments. Another equally
        important comparison is the risk-adjusted return. It is important to know
        that the return from an investment is not only better than a more
        conservative investment, but is also better on a risk-adjusted basis. This
        permits the investor to determine whether or not the return was worth the
        risk that was undertaken.

        Treynor, Sharpe, and Jensen performance measures are possible
        methods of comparing risk adjusted returns.

10.   **Weighted Average Return.**
        The Weighted Average Return represents the return for a set of
        securities, such as a portfolio, where each return is weighted by the
        proportion of the security to the entire group or portfolio.

EXHIBIT 15: INVESTMENTS - FORMULAS
✓ Denotes formula that will likely be provided on exam.

(See EXHIBIT 16 after this section for actual formulae provided on the exam)

CAPITAL ASSET PRICING MODEL (CAPM)

Capital Market Line (CML)

✓ R_p = $R_f + [(R_m-R_f)/\sigma_m]^*\sigma_p$

R_p =   The return of the portfolio.

R_f =   The risk free rate of return.

R_m =   The return on the market.

(R_m-R_f) =   The return from the market that exceeds the risk free rate of return.

σ_m =   The standard deviation of the market.

σ_p =   The standard deviation of the portfolio.

Security Market Line (SML)

✓ R_s = $R_f + \beta (R_m - R_f)$

R_s =   The return for a stock.

R_f =   The risk free rate of return.

β =   Beta, which is a measure of the systematic risk associated with a particular stock.

(R_m-R_f) =   The risk premium, which is the additional return of the market over the risk free rate of return.

Characteristic Line (CL)

R_j = $\alpha_j + \beta_j * R_m + e$

R_j =   Return for asset j.

α_j =   Y intercept or constant term.

β_j =   The slope of the line (beta).

R_m =   Rate of return for the market.

e =   Error term from the analysis.

ARBITRAGE PRICING THEORY (APT)

Arbitrage Pricing Theory (APT)

✓ $R \quad = \quad a_0 + b_1F_1 + b_2F_2 + \ldots + b_nF_n + e$

R	$=$	The return from the security.
a_0	$=$	The return that is expected for all securities when the value of all factors is zero. In some cases, this is called the expected return.
b_n	$=$	The sensitivity of the security to factor F_n.
F_2	$=$	The factor that affects the security, such as GNP of 3%.
e	$=$	The return that is unique to the security. It is also called an error term in some cases. **Note:** This error term should drop out if all relevant factors are captured by the equation.

MEASURES OF RISK

Beta

$$\beta_p \quad = \quad [\sigma_p / \sigma_m] * r_{pm}$$

β_p	$=$	Beta.
σ_p	$=$	Standard deviation of the portfolio.
σ_m	$=$	Standard deviation of the market.
r_{pm}	$=$	Correlation coefficient between the portfolio and the market.

Weighted Average Beta

$$\beta_w \quad = \quad \sum_{i=1}^{N} \left[\beta_i \times \%_i \right]$$

β_w	$=$	Weighted average.
β_i	$=$	Return for security i.
$\%_i$	$=$	Portion of security i to total portfolio.
N	$=$	Number of securities.

Expected Rate of Return

$$E(r) \quad = \quad P_1(R_1) + P_2(R_2) + ... + P_t(R_t)$$

$E(r)$	=	The expected return.
P_1	=	The probability assigned to the first rate or return.
R_1	=	The first rate of return.
t	=	The number of events that are being examined.

Standard Deviation of Forecasted Returns

✓ $$\sigma \quad = \quad Var.(r)^{1/2} = [P_1[r_1 - E(r)]^2 + P_2[r_2 - E(r)]^2 + ... + P_t[r_t - E(r)]^2]^{\frac{1}{2}}$$

$E(r)$	=	Expected return (calculated).
r_t	=	Forecasted return for outcome t.
P_t	=	Probability of outcome t.
σ	=	Standard deviation.

Standard Deviation of Historical Returns

✓ $$\sigma = \left[\sum_{i=1}^{n} (r_i - \bar{r})^2 \ / \ (n - 1) \right]^{\frac{1}{2}}$$

σ	=	Standard deviation.
n	=	Number of observations.
r_i	=	Actual return for period i.
$\bar{r}$	=	Average return.

Variance of a Two Security Portfolio

✓ σ^2 = $W_A^2\,\sigma_A^2 + W_B^2\,\sigma_B^2 + 2W_AW_B[\sigma_A\sigma_B r_{AB}]$

σ^2 = Variance.

σ = Standard deviation.

W_A = The percent of the portfolio invested in security A.

W_B = The percent of the portfolio invested in security B.

$[\sigma_A\sigma_B r_{AB}]$ = Covariance between security A & B.

r_{AB} = Correlation coefficient.

> **Note:** W_A plus W_B must sum to 100%.

Duration (Example)

Bond:

PV	=	$974.23
N	=	3
i	=	8%
PMT	=	$70
FV	=	$1,000.00

Duration Calculation			
Year	Cash Flow	Year x Cash Flow	PV @ 8%
1	$ 70	$70	$ 64.81
2	70	140	120.03
3	1,070	3,210	2,548.20
	$1,210	N/A	$2,733.04

Duration = $2,733.04 ÷ $974.23 = 2.8 years

Change in Price Using Duration

✓ $\dfrac{\Delta P}{P} = \dfrac{-D}{1 + YTM} \times \Delta YTM$

$\dfrac{\Delta P}{P}$ = Percent change in price of a bond

D = Duration

YTM = Yield to Maturity

PERFORMANCE MEASURES

The Sharpe Performance Index

✓ $S(p) = \dfrac{(Rp - Rf)}{\sigma}$

$S(p)$ = Sharpe Performance Measure for portfolio p.

Rp = The average rate of return for a given time period.

Rf = The risk free rate of return during the same time period.

σ = The standard deviation of the rate of return for portfolio p during the same time interval.

The Treynor Performance Measure

✓ $T_p = \dfrac{(Rp - Rf)}{B_p}$

T_p = Treynor Performance Measure for portfolio p.

R_p = The average rate of return for a given time period.

Rf = The risk free rate of return during the same time period.

B_p = Beta for the same period or the slope of the portfolio's characteristic line during the period.

The Jensen Model

$$(R_p - R_f) = \alpha_p + \beta_p[R_m - R_f] + e$$

$(R_p\text{-}R_f)$	=	The return that is earned solely for bearing risk.
α_p	=	Alpha, which represents the return that is able to be earned above or below an unmanaged portfolio with identical market risk.
β_p	=	Beta, which is the measure of systematic or market risk.
R_m	=	The return on the market.
R_f	=	The risk free rate of return.
e	=	The error term.

The Jensen Performance Index

✓ α_p = $R_p - [R_f + \beta_p(R_m - R_f)]$

RATES OF RETURN

Single Period Rate of Return

$$\frac{(SP - PP + CF)}{PP}$$

SP	=	The sales price for the asset.
PP	=	The initial purchase price of the asset.
CF	=	Any cash flows that occur, such as dividends, interest or other income.

Internal Rate of Return (IRR)

$$P_0 = \frac{CF_1}{(1 + k)^1} + \frac{CF_2}{(1 + k)^2} + \cdots + \frac{CF_t}{(1 + k)^t}$$

P_0	=	The value of the security today.
CF_t	=	The cash flow for period t.
k	=	The discount rate based on the security type.
t	=	The number of cash flows to be evaluated.

Yield To Maturity

$$P_0 = \frac{CF_1}{(1+k)^1} + \frac{CF_2}{(1+k)^2} + \cdots + \frac{CF_t}{(1+k)^t}$$

P_0	=	The value of the security today.
CF_t	=	The cash flow for period t.
k	=	The discount rate based on a the security type.
t	=	The number of cash flows to be evaluated.

Yield to Call (YTC)

$$P_0 = \frac{CF_1}{(1+k)^1} + \frac{CF_2}{(1+k)^2} + \cdots + \frac{CF_t}{(1+k)^t}$$

P_0	=	The value of the security today.
CF_t	=	The cash flow for period t.
k	=	The discount rate based on a the security type.
t	=	The number of cash flows to be evaluated.

Arithmetic

$$\bar{x} = \frac{\left[\sum_{i=1}^{N} r_i\right]}{N}$$

$\bar{x}$	=	Arithmetic return.
N	=	Number of observations.
r_i	=	Actual return for the period.

Time Weighted

$$P_0 = \frac{CF_1}{(1+k)^1} + \frac{CF_2}{(1+k)^2} + \cdots + \frac{CF_t}{(1+k)^t}$$

P_0 = The value of the security today.

CF_t = The cash flow for period t.

k = The discount rate based on a the security type.

t = The number of cash flows to be evaluated.

> **Note:** Time weighted return considers the cash flows of the investment only. It does not consider the cash flows of the investor.

Geometric

$$GR = [(1 + R_1)(1 + R_2)...(1 + R_N)]^{1/N} - 1$$

GR = Geometric return.

R_N = Return for each period.

N = Number of periods.

After-tax Rate of Return

Tax Adjusted Return = $R(1 - TR)$

R = Real return.

TR = Tax rate.

Inflation Adjusted Rate of Return

$$R_i = [((1 + R) \div (1 + IR)) - 1] \times 100$$

R_i = Inflation adjusted return.

R = Earnings rate.

IR = Inflation rate.

Weighted Average Return

$$\bar{x}_w = \sum_{i=1}^{N} \left[R_i \times \%_i \right]$$

$\bar{x}_w$ = Weighted average.

R_i = Return for security i.

$\%_i$ = Portion of security i to total portfolio.

N = Number of securities.

VALUATION MODELS

The Basic Present Value (Valuation) Model

$$P_0 = \frac{CF_1}{(1 + k)^1} + \frac{CF_2}{(1 + k)^2} + \cdots + \frac{CF_t}{(1 + k)^t}$$

P_0 = The value of the security today.

CF_t = The cash flow for period t.

k = The discount rate based on the type of security and risk level of the investment.

t = The number of cash flows to be evaluated.

Constant Dividend Growth Model

✓ $$P_0 = \frac{D_1}{k - g}$$

P_0 = Price for the security.

D_1 = The dividend paid at period 1.

k = The investors required rate of return.

g = The growth rate of the dividends. The growth rate can be negative, positive or zero. See perpetuities for a zero growth rate.

Capitalized Earnings

$$V = \frac{E}{R_d}$$

V	=	The value of the company or firm.
E	=	The earnings used to value the firm.
R_d	=	The discount rate.

Perpetuity

$$P_0 = \frac{D_1}{k}$$

P_0	=	Price of the security.
D	=	The dividend paid per period.
k	=	Investors required rate of return.

Conversion Factor

✓ CV = $[1{,}000 \div CP] \times P_s$

CV	=	Conversion value.
CP	=	Conversion price of stock.
P_s	=	Current price of stock.

Note: Bond face = $1,000.

EXHIBIT 16: FORMULA PAGE PROVIDED ON CFP® CERTIFICATION EXAMINATION

$$V = \frac{D_1}{r-g}$$

$$T_i = \frac{r_p - r_f}{B_p}$$

$$r = \frac{D_1}{P} + g$$

$$Si = \frac{r_p - r_f}{\sigma_p}$$

$$r_p = r_f + \sigma_p \left(\frac{r_m - r_f}{\sigma_m} \right)$$

$$a_p = r_p - [r_f + (r_m - r_f)B_p]$$

$$r_i = r_f + (r_m - r_f)B_i$$

$$Dur = \frac{\sum_{i=1}^{n} \frac{C_i(t)}{(1+i)^t}}{\sum_{i=1}^{n} \frac{C_i}{(1+i)^t}}$$

$$r_i = a_i + b_1 F_1 + b_2 F_2 + b_3 F_3 + e_i$$

-OR-

$$Dur = \frac{1+y}{y} - \frac{(1+y) + T(c-y)}{c[(1+y)^T - 1] + y}$$

$$\sigma = \sqrt{\frac{\sum_{i=1}^{n} (r_i - \bar{r})^2}{n-1}}$$

$$\frac{\Delta P}{P} = -D \left[\frac{\Delta(1+y)}{1+y} \right]$$

$$COV_{ij} = \sigma_i \times \sigma_j \times corr.coeff._{ij}$$

$$CV = \left(\frac{1,000}{CP} \right) P_s$$

$$\sigma_p = \sqrt{\sum_{i=1}^{N} W_i^2 \sigma_i^2 + \sum_{i=1}^{N} \sum_{j=1}^{N} W_i W_j Cov_{ij}}$$

EXHIBIT 17: TAX - RATE SCHEDULES (1998)

Single – Schedule X

If taxable income is: Over	But not over	The tax is:	Of the amount over --
$0	$25,350	-------------- 15%	$0
$25,350	$61,400	$3,802.50 + 28%	$25,350
$61,400	$128,100	$13,896.50 + 31%	$61,400
$128,100	$278,450	$34,573.50 + 36%	$128,100
$278,450	------------	$88,699.50 + 39.6%	$278,450

Head of Household – Schedule Z

If taxable income is: Over	But not over	The tax is:	Of the amount over --
$0	$33,950	-------------- 15%	$0
$33,950	$87,700	$5,092.50 + 28%	$33,950
$87,700	$142,000	$20,142.50 + 31%	$87,700
$142,000	$278,450	$36,975.50 + 36%	$142,000
$278,450	------------	$86,097.50 + 39.6%	$278,450

Married Filing Jointly or Qualifying Widow(er) – Schedule Y-1

If taxable income is: Over	But not over	The tax is:	Of the amount over --
$0	$42,350	-------------- 15%	$0
$42,350	$102,300	$6,352.50 + 28%	$42,350
$102,300	$155,950	$23,138.50 + 31%	$102,300
$155,950	$278,450	$39,770.00 + 36%	$155,950
$278,450	------------	$83,870.00 + 39.6%	$278,450

Married Filing Separately – Schedule Y-2

If taxable income is: Over	But not over	The tax is:	Of the amount over --
$0	$21,175	-------------- 15%	$0
$21,175	$51,150	$3,176.25 + 28%	$21,175
$51,150	$77,975	$11,569.25 + 31%	$51,150
$77,975	$139,225	$19,885.00 + 36%	$77,975
$139,225	------------	$41,935.00 + 39.6%	$139,225

EXHIBIT 18: TAX - STANDARD DEDUCTION AMOUNT & ADDITIONAL DEDUCTION

Filing Status	Standard Deduction		Additional Standard Deduction	
	1998	Expected 1999	1998	Expected 1999
Single	$4,250	$4,350	$1,050	$1,050
Married, filing jointly	$7,100	$7,300	$ 850	$ 850
Qualifying widow(er)	$7,100	$7,300	$ 850	$ 850
Head of household	$6,250	$6,400	$1,050	$1,050
Married, filing separately	$3,550	$3,650	$ 850	$ 850

EXHIBIT 19: TAX - FORMULA FOR INDIVIDUALS

Income (broadly conceived)	$xx,xxx
Less: Exclusions	(x,xxx)
Gross Income	$xx,xxx
Less: Deductions for Adjusted Gross Income	(x,xxx)
Adjusted Gross Income (AGI)	$xx,xxx
Less: The Greater of:	
Total Itemized Deductions or Standard Deduction	(x,xxx)
Less: Personal and Dependency Exemptions	(x,xxx)
Taxable Income	$xx,xxx

EXHIBIT 20: TAX - DEPENDENCY EXEMPTION (1998)

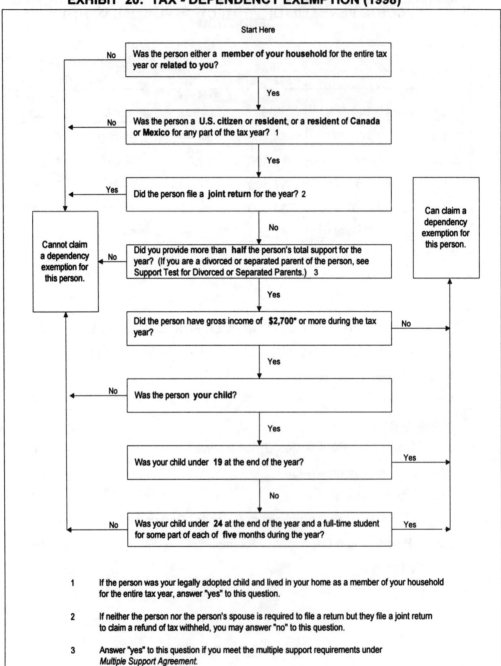

1   If the person was your legally adopted child and lived in your home as a member of your household
    for the entire tax year, answer "yes" to this question.

2   If neither the person nor the person's spouse is required to file a return but they file a joint return
    to claim a refund of tax withheld, you may answer "no" to this question.

3   Answer "yes" to this question if you meet the multiple support requirements under
    Multiple Support Agreement.

(IRS Publication 17)

*The 1999 dependency exemption is $2,800.

EXHIBIT 21: TAX - SECTION 79 COSTS FOR GROUP TERM INSURANCE COSTS PER $1,000 OF PROTECTION FOR ONE MONTH

AGE	COST
Under 30	$0.08
30 through 34	$0.09
35 through 39	$0.11
40 through 44	$0.17
45 through 49	$0.29
50 through 54	$0.48
55 through 59	$0.75
60 through 64	$1.17
65 through 69	$2.10
70 or older	$3.76

EXHIBIT 22: TAX - SECTION 179 MAXIMUM WRITE OFFS

Tax Year Beginning In	Maximum Section 179
1998	$18,500
1999	$19,000
2000	$20,000
2001 or 2002	$24,000
2003 and thereafter	$25,000

**EXHIBIT 23:   RETIREMENT - COMPARISON OF DEFINED BENEFIT,
DEFINED CONTRIBUTION,   AND CASH BALANCE PLANS**

	Typical Defined Benefit Plan DB	Typical Defined Contribution Plan DC	Cash Balance Plan CB
Contribution	Actuarially determined	Percentage of salary (could be age weighted)	Percentage of salary (actuarially determined)
Investment Risk	Employer	Employee	Employer
Size of Work Force	Any size	Any size	Large
Investment Earnings	Employer responsible	Variable	Guaranteed
Social Security Integration	Yes	Yes*	Yes
Pension Benefit Guarantee Corporation Insurance	Yes	No	Yes
401(k) Feature	No	Available in profit sharing plan	No
Favors Older Entrants	Yes	No	No
Administrative Cost	Generally higher than DC Plans due to actuary and insurance	Generally lower than DB Plans	Generally higher than DC Plans due to actuary and insurance

*ESOPs are not eligible for integration.

EXHIBIT 24: RETIREMENT - ACP/ADP GENERAL RULES (Simplified)

If ADP for NHC:	Maximum ADP for HC is:
≤ 2%	2 x ADP of NHC
≥ 2%, but ≤ 8%	2% + ADP of NHC
> 8%	1.25 x ADP of NHC

NHC = Non-highly compensated

HC = Highly compensated

EXHIBIT 25: RETIREMENT - TARGET BENEFIT ILLUSTRATION

Assume that a business owner is age 50, earns $160,000 per year, and selects a benefit formula equal to 135.5% of compensation reduced by 1/25th for each year of participation less than 25 years. The plan will also benefit one employee age 25 earning $18,000 per year. The first year deposit is determined as follows, assuming a normal retirement age of 65 and 8.5% interest.

	Business Owner	Employee
Age	50	25
Compensation	$160,000	$18,000
Target Benefit	$130,000*	$24,390**
Factor (age)	2.338	0.304
PV of Benefit	$303,940	$7,415
Factor	0.1075	0.0812
Theoretical Contribution	$32,674	$602
415 Limit (25% or $30,000)	$30,000	$4,500
Top-heavy Minimum	$0	$540
(3% of compensation)		
Actual Contribution	$30,000	$602
Contribution Rate	18.75%	3.34%
Percent of Contribution	98%	2%

*The benefit for the business owner is 135.5% x $160,000 x (15 ÷ 25) = $130,000.

**Benefit for employee is 135.5% of $18,000 or $24,390.

EXHIBIT 26: RETIREMENT - AGE-BASED PROFIT SHARING PLAN ILLUSTRATION

Assume that a business owner is age 50, earns $160,000 per year, and elects to make a maximum contribution to a discretionary age-based profit sharing plan. The plan will also benefit one employee, age 25, earning $18,000 per year.

	Business Owner	Employee	Total
Age	50	25	
Compensation	$160,000	$18,000	$178,000
Adjustment Factor @ 8.5%	0.294139	0.038265	
Age Adjusted Compensation	$47,062	$689	$47,751
Allocation	$26,315	$385	$26,700
Top-heavy Minimum	$0	$540	
(3% of compensation)			
Actual Allocation	$26,160	$540	$26,700
Contribution Rate	16.35%	3%	
Percent of Contribution	98%	2%	

The maximum deductible limit for a profit sharing plan is 15% of eligible compensation.

(15% x $178,000 = $26,700) must give employee (top heavy plan 3%) $540; therefore, business owner receives:

$26,700 - $540 = $26,160.

(Also $26,700 ÷ ($47,062 + $689) = 0.55915 x $47,062 = $26,315), (0.55915 x $689 = $385).

EXHIBIT 27: RETIREMENT - FRINGE BENEFITS BY ENTITY TYPE

Benefit	Proprietorship	Partnership	S Corp	LLC	C Corp
Qualified plan	✓	✓	✓	✓	✓
Group life	✖	✖	✖	✖	✓
Group health	Partial	Partial	Partial	Partial	✓
Group disability	✖	✖	✖	✖	✓
Medical reimb. plans	✖	✖	✖	✖	✓
Accidental death	✖	✖	✖	✖	✓
Disability income plan	✖	✖	✖	✖	✓
Employee death benefit					
Employer provided	✖	✖	✖	✖	✓
Qualified plan	✓	✓	✓	✓	✓
Cafeteria plan	✖	✖	✖	✖	✓
Deferred compensation	✖	✖	✖	✖	✓

LLC = Limited Liability Company   ✓ = Yes   ✖ = No

EXHIBIT 28:   RETIREMENT - KEOGH WORKSHEET FOR A SINGLE PROFIT SHARING PLAN OR A SINGLE MONEY PURCHASE PENSION PLAN

Line 1	Net Business Profits (From Schedule C)	$100,000
Line 2	Deduction for Self-employment Tax (From IRS Form 1040) (Given)	$6,657
Line 3	Adjusted Net Business Profits (Subtract Line 2 from Line 1)	$93,343
Line 4	Contribution Percentage (Expressed as a decimal) (Money Purchase Pension Plan, 3-25%, fixed at plan inception or Profit Sharing Plan, 0-15%, can vary each year)	0.15
Line 5	Contribution Factor (Add 1.00 to Line 4)	1.15
Line 6	Adjusted Earned Income (Divide Line 3 by Line 5)	$81,168
Line 7	Maximum Earned Income on which contributions can be based (enter $160,000)	$160,000
Line 8	Final Earned Income (The lesser of Line 6 and Line 7)	$81,168
Line 9	Preliminary Contribution Amount (Multiply Line 4 by Line 8, round down to closest dollar)	$12,175
Line 10	Maximum Dollar Contribution Amount (Enter $30,000)	$30,000
Line 11	Contribution Amount (The lesser of Line 9 and Line 10)	$12,175

EXHIBIT 29:   RETIREMENT - KEOGH WORKSHEET FOR A TANDEM PROFIT SHARING AND MONEY PURCHASE PENSION PLAN

Line 1	Net Business Profits (From Schedule C)	$160,000
Line 2	Deduction for Self-employment Tax (From IRS Form 1040) (Given)	$6,077
Line 3	Adjusted Net Business Profits (Subtract Line 2 from Line 1)	$153,923
Line 4	Money Purchase plan Contribution Percentage (Expressed as a decimal) (fixed percentage, plan established 3-25)	0.10
Line 5	Profit Sharing plan Contribution Percentage (expressed as decimal) (percentage which can vary every year, 0-15%)	0.15
Line 6	Total Contribution Percentage (expressed as decimal (between 3-25%)	0.25
Line 7	Contribution Factor (Add 1.00 to Line 4)	1.25
Line 8	Adjusted Earned Income (Divide Line 3 by Line 7)	$123,138
Line 9	Maximum Earned Income on which contributions can be based (enter $160,000)	$160,000
Line 10	Final Earned Income (lesser of Line 8 and Line 9)	$123,138
Line 11	Preliminary Money Purchase Plan Contribution Amount (Multiply Line 10 by Line 4, round down to closest dollar) (10%)	$12,314
Line 12	Maximum Money Purchase Plan Dollar Contribution Amount (Enter $30,000)	$30,000
Line 13	Money Purchase plan Contribution Amount (lesser of Line 11 and Line 12)	$12,314
Line 14	Preliminary Profit Sharing Plan Contribution Amount (Multiply Line 10 x Line 5) (15%)	$18,470
Line 15	Maximum Profit Sharing Plan Dollar Contribution Amount (Subtract Line 13 from Line 12)	$17,686
Line 16	Profit Sharing Contribution Amount (Lesser of Line 14 and Line 15)	$17,686
Line 17	Total Tandem Plan Contribution Amount (The sum of Line 13 and Line 16) (limit to $30,000	$30,000
Line 18		$30,000

Adjust to $12,000 MP and $18,000 PS = $30,000.

Note: $30,000 is DC limit (25% x $120,000 = $30,000).

EXHIBIT 30: RETIREMENT - IRA CURRENT PHASEOUT LIMITS

TRADITIONAL IRAs

Tax Year	Taxpayer Filing Status	
	Phaseout Range Single	Phaseout Range Married Filing Jointly
1997	$25,000 – 35,000	$40,000 – 50,000
1998	$30,000 – 40,000	$50,000 – 60,000
1999	$31,000 – 41,000	$51,000 – 61,000
2000	$32,000 – 42,000	$52,000 – 62,000
2001	$33,000 – 43,000	$53,000 – 63,000
2002	$34,000 – 44,000	$54,000 – 64,000
2003	$40,000 – 50,000	$60,000 – 70,000
2004	$45,000 – 55,000	$65,000 – 75,000
2005	$50,000 – 60,000	$70,000 – 80,000
2006	$50,000 – 60,000	$75,000 – 85,000
2007 and after	$50,000 – 60,000	$80,000 – 100,000

For years beginning after December 31, 1996, an individual will no longer be considered an "active participant" in an employer sponsored retirement plan solely because his or her spouse is an active participant. However, this is phased out for married taxpayers with AGI between $150,000 - $160,000 where one spouse is an "active participant".

ROTH IRAs

Taxpayer Filing Status	Modified AGI
Married filing jointly	$150,000 - $160,000
Single	$95,000 - $110,000
Married filing separately	$0 - $10,000

**EXHIBIT 31: RETIREMENT - TABLE V - ORDINARY LIFE ANNUITIES
ONE LIFE - EXPECTED RETURN MULTIPLES
(REG. SECTION 1.72-9)**

Age	Multiple	Age	Multiple	Age	Multiple
5	76.6	42	40.6	79	10.0
6	75.6	43	39.6	80	9.5
7	74.7	44	38.7	81	8.9
8	73.7	45	37.7	82	8.4
9	72.7	46	36.8	83	7.9
10	71.7	47	35.9	84	7.4
11	70.7	48	34.9	85	6.9
12	69.7	49	34.0	86	6.5
13	68.8	50	33.1	87	6.1
14	67.8	51	32.2	88	5.7
15	66.8	52	31.3	89	5.3
16	65.8	53	30.4	90	5.0
17	64.8	54	29.5	91	4.7
18	63.9	55	28.6	92	4.4
19	62.9	56	27.7	93	4.1
20	61.9	57	26.8	94	3.9
21	60.9	58	25.9	95	3.7
22	59.9	59	25.0	96	3.4
23	59.0	60	24.2	97	3.2
24	58.0	61	23.3	98	3.0
25	57.0	62	22.5	99	2.8
26	56.0	63	21.6	100	2.7
27	55.1	64	20.8	101	2.5
28	54.1	65	20.0	102	2.3
29	53.1	66	19.2	103	2.1
30	52.2	67	18.4	104	1.9
31	51.2	68	17.6	105	1.8
32	50.2	69	16.8	106	1.6
33	49.3	70	16.0	107	1.4
34	48.3	71	15.3	108	1.3
35	47.3	72	14.6	109	1.1
36	46.4	73	13.9	110	1.0
37	45.4	74	13.2	111	0.9
38	44.4	75	12.5	112	0.8
39	43.5	76	11.9	113	0.7
40	42.5	77	11.2	114	0.6
41	41.5	78	10.6	115	0.5

EXHIBIT 32: RETIREMENT - TABLE VI - ORDINARY JOINT LIFE AND LAST SURVIVOR ANNUITIES
TWO LIVES – EXPECTED RETURN MULTIPLES
(REG. SECTION 1.72-9)

Ages	65	66	67	68	69	70	71	72	73	74
65	25.0	24.6	24.2	23.8	23.4	23.1	22.8	22.5	22.2	22.0
66	24.6	24.1	23.7	23.3	22.9	22.5	22.2	21.9	21.6	21.4
67	24.2	23.7	23.2	22.8	22.4	22.0	21.7	21.3	21.0	20.8
68	23.8	23.3	22.8	22.3	21.9	21.5	21.2	20.8	20.5	20.2
69	23.4	22.9	22.4	21.9	21.5	21.1	20.7	20.3	20.0	19.6
70	23.1	22.5	22.0	21.5	21.1	20.6	20.2	19.8	19.4	19.1
71	22.8	22.2	21.7	21.2	20.7	20.2	19.8	19.4	19.0	18.6
72	22.5	21.9	21.3	20.8	20.3	19.8	19.4	18.9	18.5	18.2
73	22.2	21.6	21.0	20.5	20.0	19.4	19.0	18.5	18.1	17.7
74	22.0	21.4	20.8	20.2	19.6	19.1	18.6	18.2	17.7	17.3
75	21.8	21.1	20.5	19.9	19.3	18.8	18.3	17.8	17.3	16.9
76	21.6	20.9	20.3	19.7	19.1	18.5	18.0	17.5	17.0	16.5
77	21.4	20.7	20.1	19.4	18.8	18.3	17.7	17.2	16.7	16.2
78	21.2	20.5	19.9	19.2	18.6	18.0	17.5	16.9	16.4	15.9
79	21.1	20.4	19.7	19.0	18.4	17.8	17.2	16.7	16.1	15.6
80	21.0	20.2	19.5	18.9	18.2	17.6	17.0	16.4	15.9	15.4
81	20.8	20.1	19.4	18.7	18.1	17.4	16.8	16.2	15.7	15.1
82	20.7	20.0	19.3	18.6	17.9	17.3	16.6	16.0	15.5	14.9
83	20.6	19.9	19.2	18.5	17.8	17.1	16.5	15.9	15.3	14.7
84	20.5	19.8	19.1	18.4	17.7	17.0	16.3	15.7	15.1	14.5
85	20.5	19.7	19.0	18.3	17.6	16.9	16.2	15.6	15.0	14.4
86	20.4	19.6	18.9	18.2	17.5	16.8	16.1	15.5	14.8	14.2
87	20.4	19.6	18.8	18.1	17.4	16.7	16.0	15.4	14.7	14.1
88	20.3	19.5	18.8	18.0	17.3	16.6	15.9	15.3	14.6	14.0
89	20.3	19.5	18.7	18.0	17.2	16.5	15.8	15.2	14.5	13.9
90	20.2	19.4	18.7	17.9	17.2	16.5	15.8	15.1	14.5	13.8
91	20.2	19.4	18.6	17.9	17.1	16.4	15.7	15.0	14.4	13.7
92	20.2	19.4	18.6	17.8	17.1	16.4	15.7	15.0	14.3	13.7
93	20.1	19.3	18.6	17.8	17.1	16.3	15.6	14.9	14.3	13.6
94	20.1	19.3	18.5	17.8	17.0	16.3	15.6	14.9	14.2	13.6
95	20.1	19.3	18.5	17.8	17.0	16.3	15.6	14.9	14.2	13.5
96	20.1	19.3	18.5	17.7	17.0	16.2	15.5	14.8	14.2	13.5
97	20.1	19.3	18.5	17.7	17.0	16.2	15.5	14.8	14.1	13.5
98	20.1	19.3	18.5	17.7	16.9	16.2	15.5	14.8	14.1	13.4
99	20.0	19.2	18.5	17.7	16.9	16.2	15.5	14.7	14.1	13.4
100	20.0	19.2	18.4	17.7	16.9	16.2	15.4	14.7	14.0	13.4
101	20.0	19.2	18.4	17.7	16.9	16.1	15.4	14.7	14.0	13.3
102	20.0	19.2	18.4	17.6	16.9	16.1	15.4	14.7	14.0	13.3
103	20.0	19.2	18.4	17.6	16.9	16.1	15.4	14.7	14.0	13.3
104	20.0	19.2	18.4	17.6	16.9	16.1	15.4	14.7	14.0	13.3
105	20.0	19.2	18.4	17.6	16.8	16.1	15.4	14.6	13.9	13.3
106	20.0	19.2	18.4	17.6	16.8	16.1	15.3	14.6	13.9	13.3
107	20.0	19.2	18.4	17.6	16.8	16.1	15.3	14.6	13.9	13.2
108	20.0	19.2	18.4	17.6	16.8	16.1	15.3	14.6	13.9	13.2
109	20.0	19.2	18.4	17.6	16.8	16.1	15.3	14.6	13.9	13.2
110	20.0	19.2	18.4	17.6	16.8	16.1	15.3	14.6	13.9	13.2
111	20.0	19.2	18.4	17.6	16.8	16.0	15.3	14.6	13.9	13.2
112	20.0	19.2	18.4	17.6	16.8	16.0	15.3	14.6	13.9	13.2
113	20.0	19.2	18.4	17.6	16.8	16.0	15.3	14.6	13.9	13.2
114	20.0	19.2	18.4	17.6	16.8	16.0	15.3	14.6	13.9	13.2
115	20.0	19.2	18.4	17.6	16.8	16.0	15.3	14.6	13.9	13.2

EXHIBIT 33: RETIREMENT - INDEXED LIMITS FOR PENSION AND OTHER PLANS

	1990	1991	1992	1993	1994	1995	1996	1997	1998	1999
Defined benefit max. limit	102,582	108,963	112,221	115,641	118,800	120,000	120,000	125,000	130,000	130,000
Defined contribution plan max. limit	30,000	30,000	30,000	30,000	30,000	30,000	30,000	30,000	30,000	30,000
401k deferral limit	7,979	8,475	8,728	8,994	9,240	9,240	9,500	9,500	10,000	10,000
HC Employee – 414(q)										
- 5% owner									Any	Any
- compensation	85,485	90,803	95,518	96,368	99,000	100,000	100,000	80,000	80,000	80,000
- top paid group	56,990	60,535	62,345	64,245	66,000	66,000	66,000	N/A	N/A	N/A
- officer 50% DB limit	51,291	54,481	56,110	57,820	59,400	60,000	60,000	N/A	N/A	N/A
SEP plans										
- minimum earnings	342	363	374	385	396	400	400	N/A	N/A	N/A
- maximum earnings	209,200	222,220	228,860	235,840	150,000	150,000	150,000	Repealed	Repealed	Repealed
Excess distributions	128,228	136,204	140,276	144,551	148,500	150,000	155,000	Repealed	Repealed	Repealed
Max. compensation	209,200	222,220	228,860	235,840	150,000	150,000	150,000	160,000	160,000	160,000
S.S. Integration										
- rate	5.70	5.70	5.70	5.70	5.70	5.70	5.70	5.70	5.70	5.70
- wage base	51,300	53,400	55,500	57,600	60,600	61,200	62,700	65,400	68,400	72,600
Medicare										
- wage base	N/A	125,000	130,200	135,000	UNLIMITED	UNLIMITED	UNLIMITED	UNLIMITED	UNLIMITED	UNLIMITED
S.S. Earnings Limitation										
≤ 65						8,160	8,280	8,640	9,120	9,600
65 < 70						11,280	11,520	12,020	14,500	14,500
PBGC Limit (monthly)	2,164.77	2,250.00	2,352.27	2,437.50	2,556.82	2,569.74	2,642.05	2,761.36	2,880.68	3,051.14

EXHIBIT 34: RETIREMENT - TABLE FOR DETERMINING APPLICABLE DIVISOR FOR MDIB*

(Minimum Distribution Incidental Benefit)

AGE	APPLICABLE DIVISOR	AGE	APPLICABLE DIVISOR
70	26.2	93	8.8
71	25.3	94	8.3
72	24.4	95	7.8
73	23.5	96	7.3
74	22.7	97	6.9
75	21.8	98	6.5
76	20.9	99	6.1
77	20.1	100	5.7
78	19.2	101	5.3
79	18.4	102	5.0
80	17.6	103	4.7
81	16.8	104	4.4
82	16.0	105	4.1
83	15.3	106	3.8
84	14.5	107	3.6
85	13.8	108	3.3
86	13.1	109	3.1
87	12.4	110	2.8
88	11.8	111	2.6
89	11.1	112	2.4
90	10.5	113	2.2
91	9.9	114	2.0
92	9.4	115	1.8

*Use this table if the beneficiary is someone other than spouse.

EXHIBIT 35: RETIREMENT - SELF-EMPLOYED PERSON'S RATE TABLE

Column A	Column B
If the Plan Contribution Rate is:	The Self-employed Person's Rate is:
(shown as a %)	(shown as a decimal)
1..........	0.009901
2..........	0.019608
3..........	0.029126
4..........	0.038462
5..........	0.047619
6..........	0.056604
7..........	0.065421
8..........	0.074074
9..........	0.082569
10..........	0.090909
11..........	0.099099
12..........	0.107143
13..........	0.115044
14..........	0.122807
→ 15*........	0.130435* ←
16..........	0.137931
17..........	0.145299
18..........	0.152542
19..........	0.159664
20..........	0.166667
21..........	0.173554
22..........	0.180328
23..........	0.186992
24..........	0.193548
→ 25**........	0.200000** ←

*The deduction for annual employer contributions to a SEP or profit sharing plan cannot exceed 15% of the common law employee participants' compensation, or 13.0435% of the self-employed compensation (figured without deducting contributions) from the business that has the plan. Factor is calculated as follows: (0.15 ÷ 1.15 = 0.130435).

**Factor is calculated as follows: (0.25 ÷ 1.25 = 0.20)

EXHIBIT 36: ESTATES - ASSETS PASSING THROUGH AND AROUND THE PROBATE PROCESS

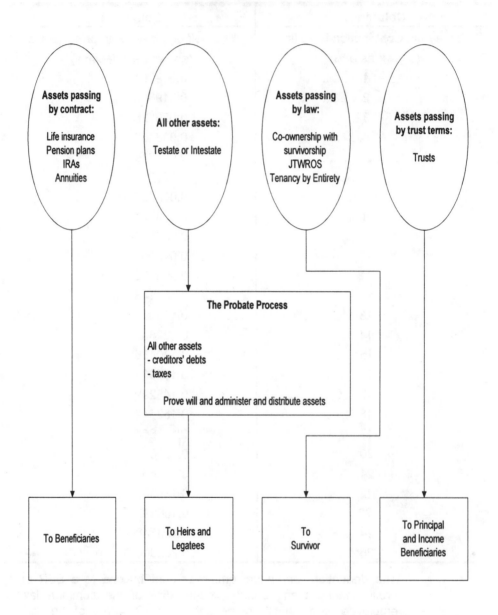